Guitar Chord Songbook

Country Hits

ISBN 978-1-4950-0817-7

7777 W. Bluemound Rd. P.O. Box 13819 Milwaukee, WI 53213

Visit Hal Leonard Online at
www.halleonard.com

Contents

Ain't Nothing 'Bout You

Words and Music by
Tom Shapiro and
Rivers Rutherford

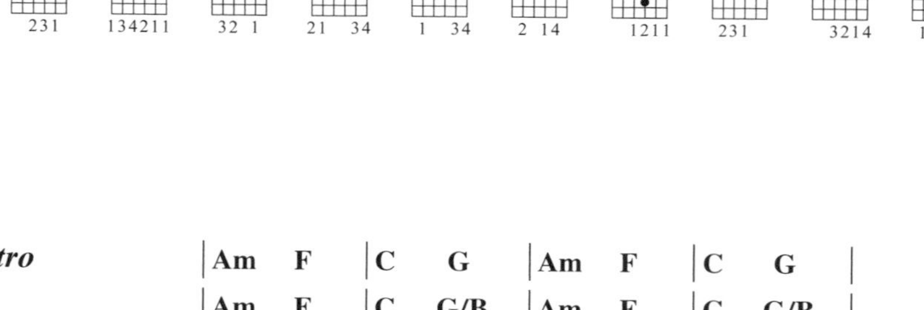

Intro

| Am F | C G | Am F | C G |
| Am F | C G/B | Am F | C G/B |

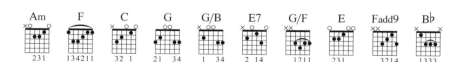

Verse 1

```
Am                            E7                  F
   Once I thought that love was somethin' I could never do.
      C                 G/B
Never knew that I could feel this much.
Am                      E7                     F
   But this yearnin' in the deep part of my heart for you
  C               G/B        F
Is more than a re - action to your touch.
        G/F           F         E
It's a per - fect passion    and I can't get enough.
```

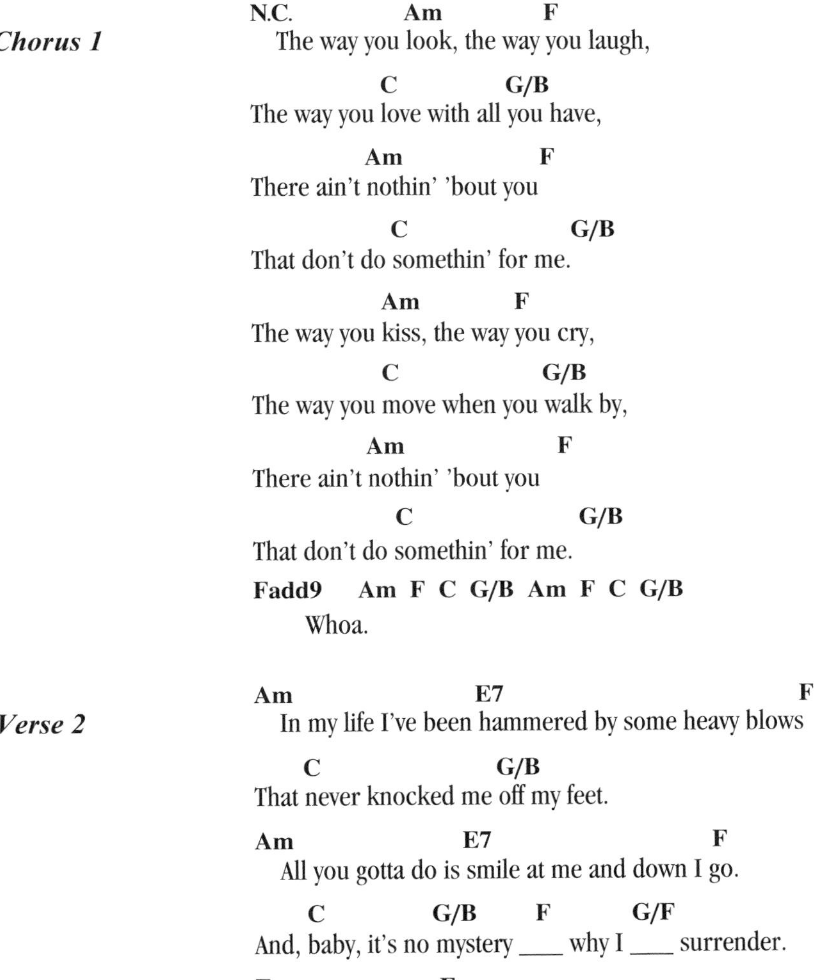

Chorus 1

```
N.C.            Am             F
   The way you look, the way you laugh,
                C              G/B
The way you love with all you have,
             Am                 F
There ain't nothin' 'bout you
                C                    G/B
That don't do somethin' for me.
                Am             F
The way you kiss, the way you cry,
                C                 G/B
The way you move when you walk by,
             Am                   F
There ain't nothin' 'bout you
                C                    G/B
That don't do somethin' for me.
Fadd9   Am  F  C  G/B  Am  F  C  G/B
     Whoa.
```

Verse 2

```
Am                        E7                              F
   In my life I've been hammered by some heavy blows
    C                      G/B
That never knocked me off my feet.
Am                     E7                         F
   All you gotta do is smile at me and down I go.
    C            G/B        F          G/F
And, baby, it's no mystery ___ why I ___ surrender.
F                  E
   Girl, you've got ev'rything.
```

Chorus 2

```
N.C.            Am           F
   The way you look, the way you laugh,

              C            G/B
The way you love with all you have,

            Am                F
There ain't nothin' 'bout you

               C                    G/B
That don't do somethin' for me.

              Am           F
The way you kiss, the way you cry,

              C                G/B
The way you move when you walk by,

            Am                F
There ain't nothin' 'bout you

               C                   G/B
That don't do somethin' for me.
```

Bridge

```
Bb                              F
   I love your attitude, your rose tattoo,

     C              Bb
Your ev'ry thought,    your smile, your lips

     E                                  Am  F  C  G/B  Am  F  C  G/B
And, girl, the list goes on and on and on.
```

Chorus 3

```
                Am   N.C.    F   N.C.
The way you look, the way you laugh,
                C    N.C.    G   N.C.
The way you love with all you have,
               Am      N.C.      F  N.C.
There ain't nothin' 'bout you
                 Gsus4              G
That don't do somethin' for me.
                Am              F
The way you kiss, the way you cry,
                C                   G/B
The way you move when you walk by,
               Am                F
There ain't nothin' 'bout you
                 C                   G/B
That don't do somethin' for me.
                Am              F
The way you look, the way you laugh,
                C              G/B
The way you love with all you have,
      Am    F
Your dance, your drive,
    C              G/B  Am  F
You make me feel alive.
C  G/B             Am             F
         The way you talk, the way you tease,
   C           G/B
By now I think you see
               Am                F
There ain't nothin' 'bout you
                 C                   G/B
That don't do somethin' for me.
```

Outro

||: **Am F** | **C G/B** :|| ***Repeat and fade***

All I Want to Do

Words and Music by Bobby Olen Pinson,
Kristian Bush and Jennifer Nettles

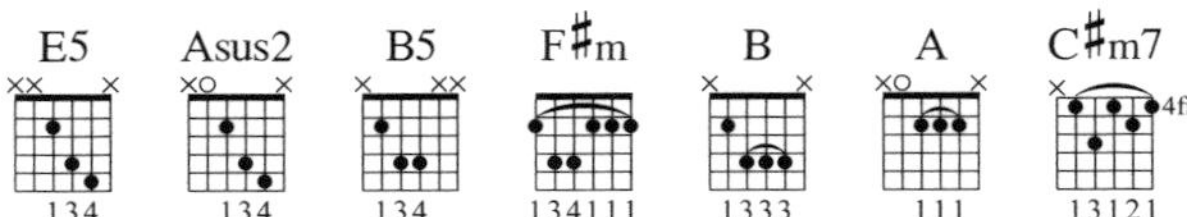

Intro | **E5** | | **Asus2** | **N.C.** |

Verse 1

E5
I don't wanna get up, baby, let's turn off the phone.

Asus2
I don't wanna go to work today or even put my makeup on.

E5 **B5**
I've got better things to do than my "To Do" list anyway,

Asus2
Hide under the covers and waste away the day.

B5
Let's just lay here and be lazy, baby, drive me crazy.

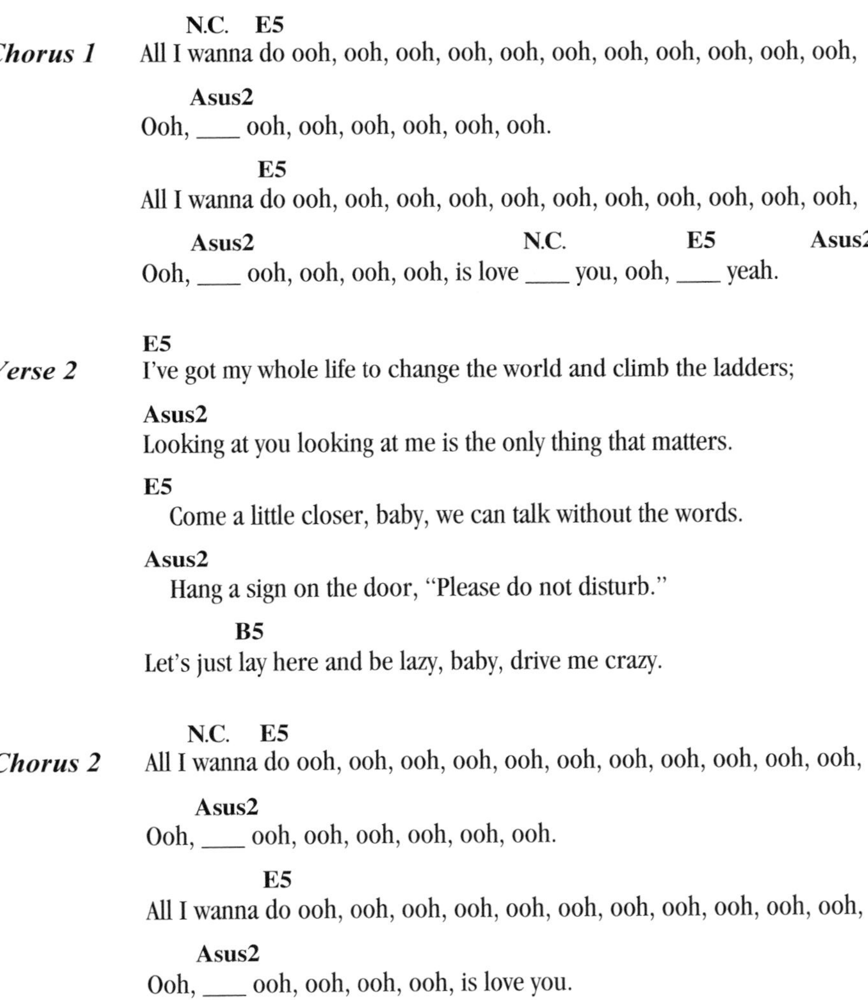

N.C. E5
Chorus 1 All I wanna do ooh, ooh, ooh, ooh, ooh, ooh, ooh, ooh, ooh, ooh, ooh,

Asus2
Ooh, ___ ooh, ooh, ooh, ooh, ooh, ooh.

E5
All I wanna do ooh, ooh, ooh, ooh, ooh, ooh, ooh, ooh, ooh, ooh, ooh,

Asus2 N.C. E5 Asus2
Ooh, ___ ooh, ooh, ooh, ooh, is love ___ you, ooh, ___ yeah.

E5
Verse 2 I've got my whole life to change the world and climb the ladders;

Asus2
Looking at you looking at me is the only thing that matters.

E5
Come a little closer, baby, we can talk without the words.

Asus2
Hang a sign on the door, "Please do not disturb."

B5
Let's just lay here and be lazy, baby, drive me crazy.

N.C. E5
Chorus 2 All I wanna do ooh, ooh, ooh, ooh, ooh, ooh, ooh, ooh, ooh, ooh, ooh,

Asus2
Ooh, ___ ooh, ooh, ooh, ooh, ooh, ooh.

E5
All I wanna do ooh, ooh, ooh, ooh, ooh, ooh, ooh, ooh, ooh, ooh, ooh,

Asus2
Ooh, ___ ooh, ooh, ooh, ooh, is love you.

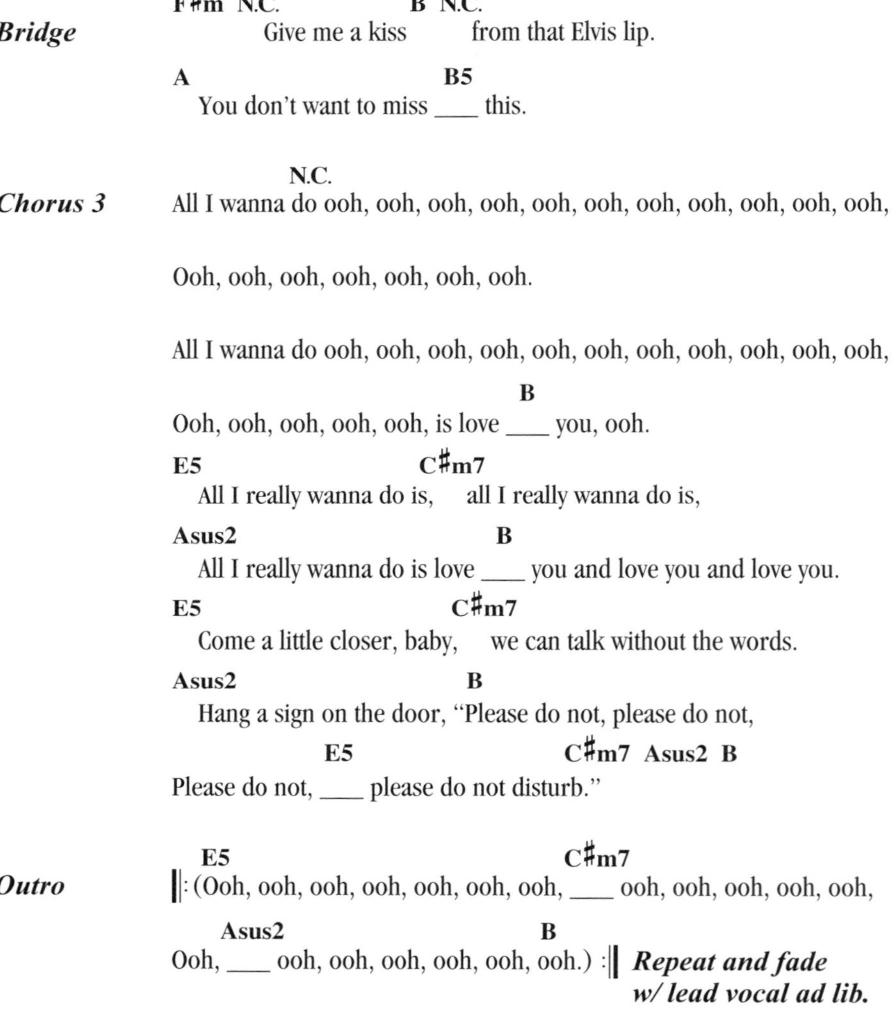

Bridge

F♯m N.C. B N.C.
Give me a kiss from that Elvis lip.

A B5
You don't want to miss ___ this.

Chorus 3

N.C.
All I wanna do ooh, ooh, ooh, ooh, ooh, ooh, ooh, ooh, ooh, ooh, ooh,

Ooh, ooh, ooh, ooh, ooh, ooh, ooh.

All I wanna do ooh, ooh, ooh, ooh, ooh, ooh, ooh, ooh, ooh, ooh, ooh,

B
Ooh, ooh, ooh, ooh, ooh, is love ___ you, ooh.

E5 C♯m7
All I really wanna do is, all I really wanna do is,

Asus2 B
All I really wanna do is love ___ you and love you and love you.

E5 C♯m7
Come a little closer, baby, we can talk without the words.

Asus2 B
Hang a sign on the door, "Please do not, please do not,

E5 C♯m7 Asus2 B
Please do not, ___ please do not disturb."

Outro

E5 C♯m7
‖: (Ooh, ooh, ooh, ooh, ooh, ooh, ooh, ___ ooh, ooh, ooh, ooh, ooh,

Asus2 B
Ooh, ___ ooh, ooh, ooh, ooh, ooh, ooh.) :‖ ***Repeat and fade w/ lead vocal ad lib.***

Beautiful Mess

Words and Music by Sonny LeMaire,
Clay Mills and Shane Minor

(Capo 1st fret)

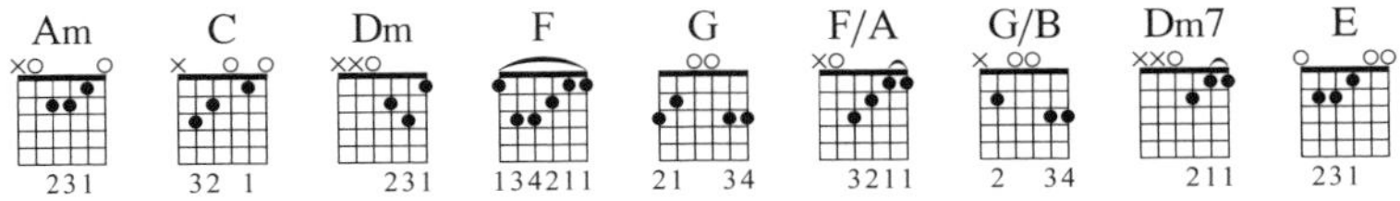

Am C Dm F G F/A G/B Dm7 E

231 32 1 231 134211 21 34 3211 2 34 211 231

Intro ‖: **Am** | | **C** | :‖

Verse 1

Am **C**
Goin' out of my mind these days

Am **C**
Like I'm walkin' 'round in a haze.

Dm **F**
I can't think straight, I can't concentrate

And I need a shave.

Verse 2

Am **C**
I go to work and I look tired.

Am **C**
The boss man says, "Son, you're gonna get fired.

Dm
This ain't your style."

F **Am**
And behind my coffee cup I just smile.

Chorus 1

C   G
What a beautiful mess, what a beautiful mess ____ I'm in.

                F
Spendin' all ____ my time with you,

                        G   F/A   G/B
There's nothin' else ____ I'd rath - er do.

C   G
What a sweet addiction that I'm caught ____ up in.

            F
'Cause I ____ can't get enough,

                    Am   G   F
Can't stop the hun - ger for ____ your love.

                                                    Am
What a beautiful, what a beautiful mess ____ I'm in.

     C   Am   C
Ah, ah.

Verse 3

Am   C
This mornin' put salt in my coffee.

Am   C
I put my shoes on the wrong feet.

                         Dm
I'm losin' my mind, I swear.

                          F   Am
It might be the death ____ of me, but I don't ____ care.

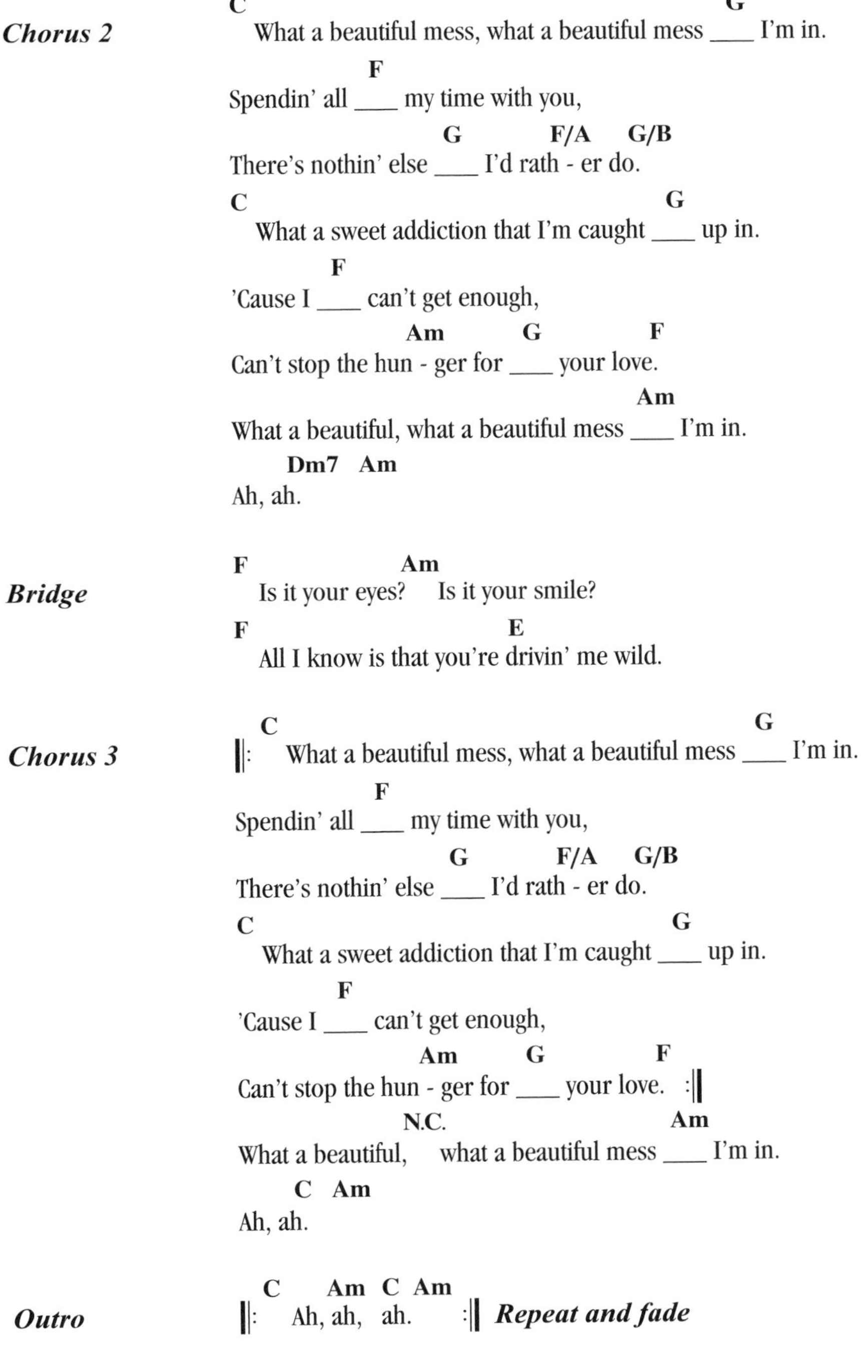

Chorus 2

C G
What a beautiful mess, what a beautiful mess ___ I'm in.
F
Spendin' all ___ my time with you,
G F/A G/B
There's nothin' else ___ I'd rath - er do.
C G
What a sweet addiction that I'm caught ___ up in.
F
'Cause I ___ can't get enough,
Am G F
Can't stop the hun - ger for ___ your love.
Am
What a beautiful, what a beautiful mess ___ I'm in.
Dm7 Am
Ah, ah.

Bridge

F Am
Is it your eyes? Is it your smile?
F E
All I know is that you're drivin' me wild.

Chorus 3

C G
‖: What a beautiful mess, what a beautiful mess ___ I'm in.
F
Spendin' all ___ my time with you,
G F/A G/B
There's nothin' else ___ I'd rath - er do.
C G
What a sweet addiction that I'm caught ___ up in.
F
'Cause I ___ can't get enough,
Am G F
Can't stop the hun - ger for ___ your love. :‖
N.C. Am
What a beautiful, what a beautiful mess ___ I'm in.
C Am
Ah, ah.

Outro

C Am C Am
‖: Ah, ah, ah. :‖ ***Repeat and fade***

As Good As I Once Was

Words and Music by
Toby Keith and Scotty Emerick

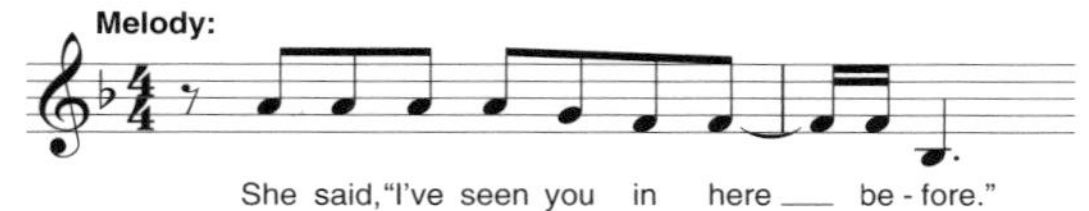

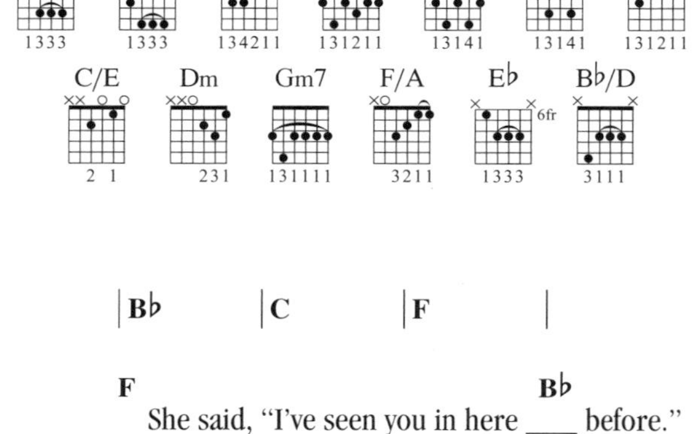

Intro | B♭ | C | F |

Verse 1

```
F                                  B♭
   She said, "I've seen you in here ___ before."
C                              F
   I said, "I've been here a time ___ or two."
                           B♭
She said, "Hello, my name is Bobby Jo.
C                     F
   Meet my twin sister Bet - ty Lou.
                          B♭
And we're both feelin' kinda wild tonight.
C                         F
   You're the only cowboy in this place.
                        G7
And if you're up for a ro - deo,
                           C7          G7  B7  C7
I'll put a big Texas smile ___ on your face."
```

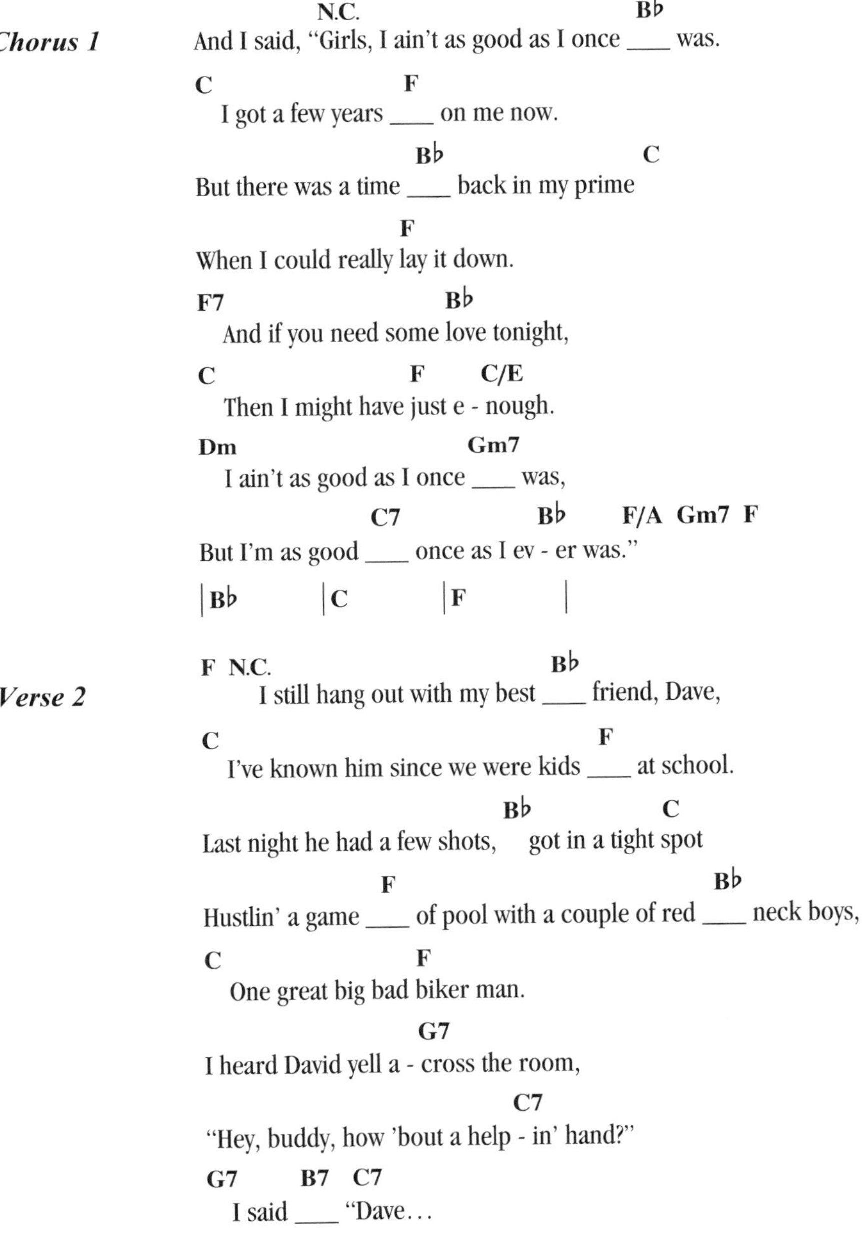

Chorus 1

N.C. Bb
And I said, "Girls, I ain't as good as I once ___ was.

C F
I got a few years ___ on me now.

Bb C
But there was a time ___ back in my prime

F
When I could really lay it down.

F7 Bb
And if you need some love tonight,

C F C/E
Then I might have just e - nough.

Dm Gm7
I ain't as good as I once ___ was,

C7 Bb F/A Gm7 F
But I'm as good ___ once as I ev - er was."

| Bb | C | F |

Verse 2

F N.C. Bb
I still hang out with my best ___ friend, Dave,

C F
I've known him since we were kids ___ at school.

Bb C
Last night he had a few shots, got in a tight spot

F Bb
Hustlin' a game ___ of pool with a couple of red ___ neck boys,

C F
One great big bad biker man.

G7
I heard David yell a - cross the room,

C7
"Hey, buddy, how 'bout a help - in' hand?"

G7 B7 C7
I said ___ "Dave…

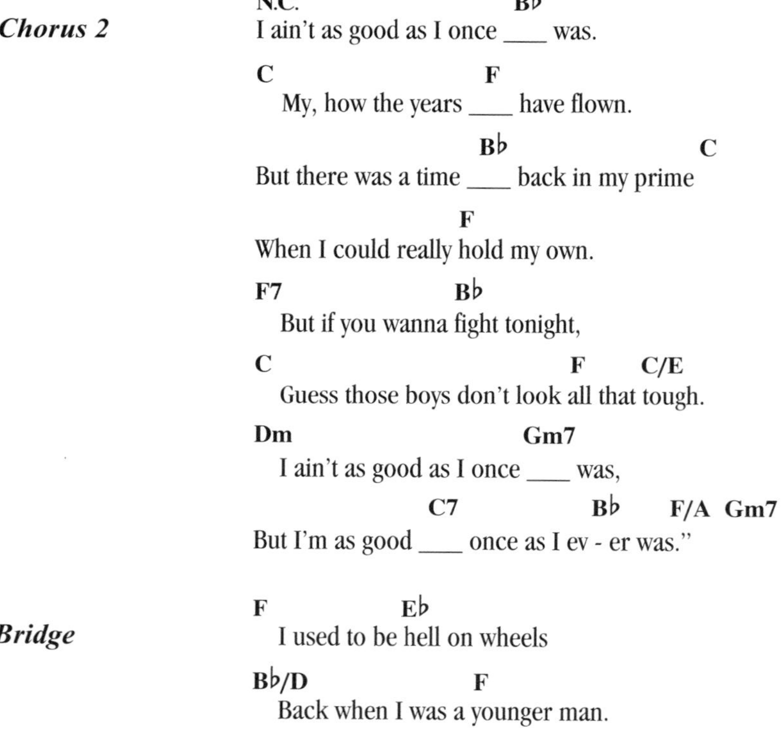

Chorus 2

N.C. Bb
I ain't as good as I once ___ was.

C F
My, how the years ___ have flown.

Bb C
But there was a time ___ back in my prime

F
When I could really hold my own.

F7 Bb
But if you wanna fight tonight,

C F C/E
Guess those boys don't look all that tough.

Dm Gm7
I ain't as good as I once ___ was,

C7 Bb F/A Gm7
But I'm as good ___ once as I ev - er was."

Bridge

F Eb
I used to be hell on wheels

Bb/D F
Back when I was a younger man.

G7
Now my body says, "You can't do this, boy."

C7 G7 B7 C7
But my pride says, "Oh, yes you can."

Chorus 3

```
N.C.                          B♭
I ain't as good as I once ___ was.
C                         F
   That's just the cold ___ hard truth.
                          B♭                    C
I still throw a few back, ___ talk a little smack
                        F
When I'm feelin' bul - letproof.
F7                        B♭
   So, don't double dog dare me now,
C                            F        C/E
   'Cause I'd have to call ___ your bluff.
Dm                           Gm7
   I ain't as good as I once ___ was,
                     C7              B♭      F/A  Gm7
But I'm as good ___ once as I ev - er was.
F                                 B♭
   May not be good as I once ___ was,
                     C               B♭      F/A  Gm7  F  B♭  C  F
But I'm as good ___ once as I ev - er was.
```

Before He Cheats

Words and Music by
Josh Kear and Chris Tompkins

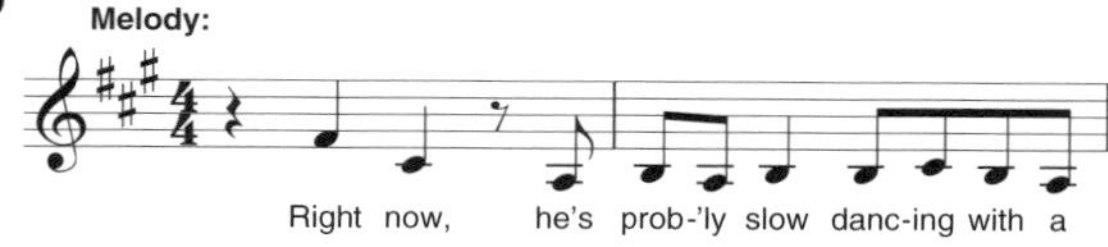

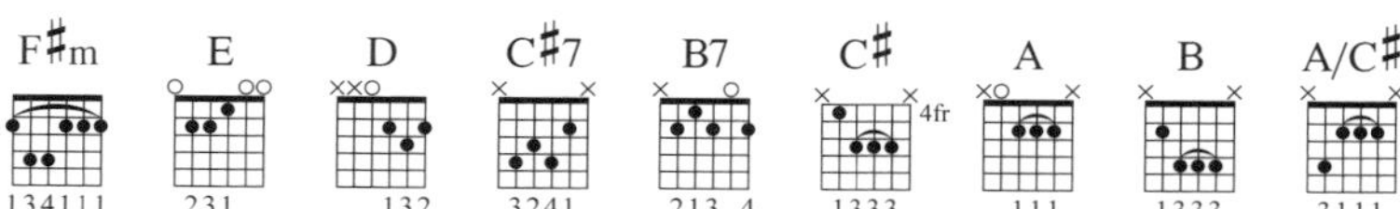

Intro

| F#m | E | D | E |
| F#m | E | D | C#7 |

Verse 1

```
F#m              E
   Right now, he's prob'ly slow dancin'
      D                                 C#7
With a bleach blonde tramp and she's prob'bly gettin' frisky.
F#m              E
   Right now, he's prob'ly buyin' her
     D                              C#7
Some fruity little drink 'cause she can't shoot whiskey.
F#m              E
   Right now, he's prob'bly up behind her
      D                          C#7                  B7
With a pool stick showing her how to shoot a combo.
                 C#
And he don't know...
```

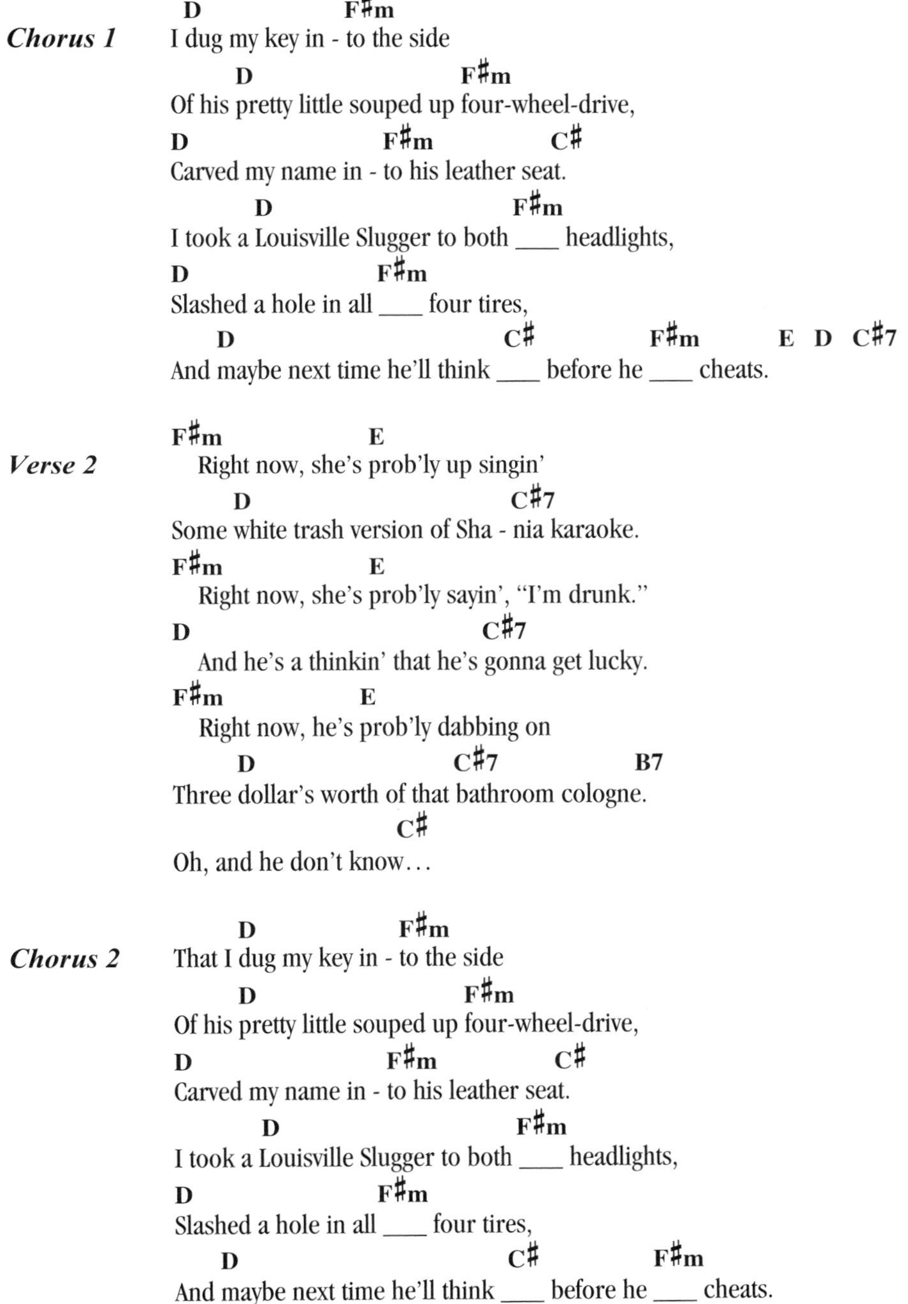

Chorus 1

D F#m
I dug my key in - to the side
D F#m
Of his pretty little souped up four-wheel-drive,
D F#m C#
Carved my name in - to his leather seat.
D F#m
I took a Louisville Slugger to both ___ headlights,
D F#m
Slashed a hole in all ___ four tires,
D C# F#m E D C#7
And maybe next time he'll think ___ before he ___ cheats.

Verse 2

F#m E
Right now, she's prob'ly up singin'
D C#7
Some white trash version of Sha - nia karaoke.
F#m E
Right now, she's prob'ly sayin', "I'm drunk."
D C#7
And he's a thinkin' that he's gonna get lucky.
F#m E
Right now, he's prob'ly dabbing on
D C#7 B7
Three dollar's worth of that bathroom cologne.
C#
Oh, and he don't know…

Chorus 2

D F#m
That I dug my key in - to the side
D F#m
Of his pretty little souped up four-wheel-drive,
D F#m C#
Carved my name in - to his leather seat.
D F#m
I took a Louisville Slugger to both ___ headlights,
D F#m
Slashed a hole in all ___ four tires,
D C# F#m
And maybe next time he'll think ___ before he ___ cheats.

Bridge

A E D
I might have saved a little trouble for the next girl,

B C♯
'Cause the next time he cheats,

F♯m E
Oh, you know it won't be on ___ me.

D C♯ F♯m E D C♯
No, ___ not on ___ me.

Chorus 3

D F♯m
'Cause I dug my key in - to the side

D F♯m
Of his pretty little souped up four-wheel-drive,

D F♯m C♯
Carved my name in - to his leather seat.

D F♯m
I took a Louisville Slugger to both ___ headlights,

D F♯m
Slashed a hole in all ___ four tires,

D C♯ B
And maybe next time he'll think ___ before he cheats.

A/C♯ D C♯
Oh, ___ maybe next time he'll think

F♯m E
Before he ___ cheats.

D E F♯m E D C♯
Oh, ___ before he ___ cheats. Oh.

Blessed

Words and Music by Brett James,
Hillary Lindsey and Troy Verges

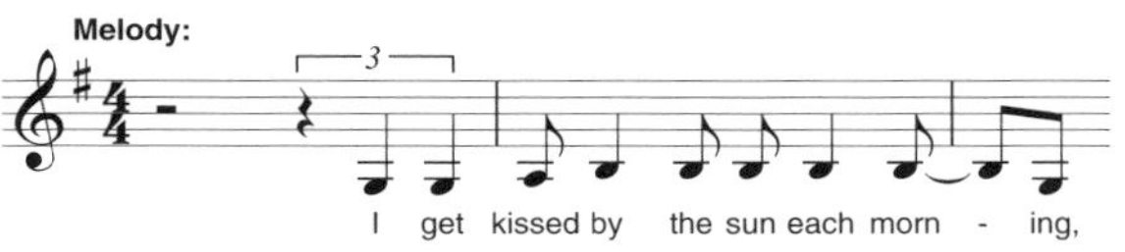

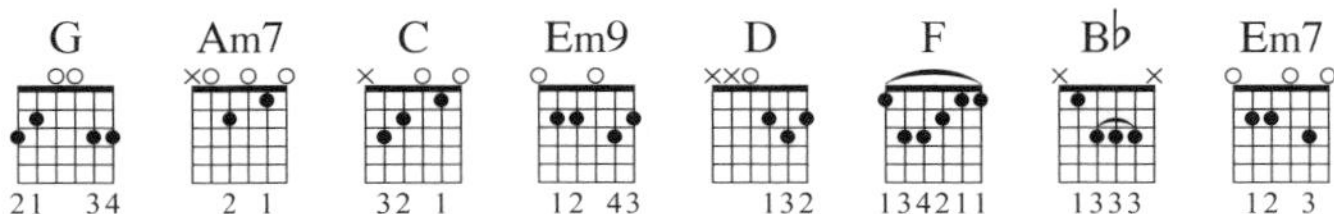

Intro

| G | | Am7 | |
| C | | G | |

Verse 1

    G
I get kissed by the sun each morning,
      Am7
Put my feet on a hardwood floor.
      C
I get to hear my children laughing
         G
Down the hall through the bedroom door.

Sometimes I sit on my front porch swing,
    Am7
Just   soakin' up the day.
 C
I think to myself, I think to myself
    G
This world is a beautiful place.

Chorus 1

G Em9
I have been blessed and I feel like I found my way.

C D
I thank God for all I've been given at the end of every day.

G Em9
I have been blessed with so much more than I deserve,

F D
To be here with the ones who love me, to love them so much it hurts.

G
I have been blessed.

Verse 2

Am7
A - cross the crowded room

C
I know you know what I'm thinkin'

G
By the way I look at you.

And when we're lying in the quiet

Am7
And no ___ words have to be said,

C
I think to myself, I think to myself,

G
"This love is a beautiful gift."

Chorus 2 *Repeat Chorus 1*

Guitar Solo

| G | | Em9 | |
| C | | D | |

Bridge

```
Bb                                 F
    When I, when I'm singin' my kids to sleep,
                  Bb              D
When I feel you holdin' me, I know
```

Chorus 3

```
        G                                   Em7
I am ___ so blessed. And I feel like I     found my way.
         C                                     D
I thank God for all I've been given at the end of every day.
              G                        Em9
I have been blessed with so much more than I deserve,
      F                                              D
To be here with the ones who love me, to love them so much it hurts.
         G                              Em9                C
I have ___ been blessed. Oh, yes, ___ I have been ___ blessed,
               D
Oh, yeah, yeah.
```

Outro

```
    G                  Em7
‖: I have been blessed,
C                   D
I have been blessed.     :‖   Repeat and fade
```

Come a Little Closer

Words and Music by
Dierks Bentley and Brett Beavers

Melody:
Come a lit - tle clos - er, ba - by,

(Capo 1st fret)

E Asus2 C♯m A Esus4 F♯m11 B

Intro | E | Asus2 | E | Asus2 |

Verse 1

E
Come a little closer, baby,

Asus2 E Asus2
I feel like layin' you ___ down

E Asus2
On a bed of sweet surren - der,

E Asus2
Where we can work it all out.

C♯m A
There ain't nothin' that love ___ can't fix.

C♯m A
Girl, it's right here at our fingertips.

E
So, come a little closer, baby,

Asus2 E Asus2
I feel like layin' you ___ down.

Verse 2

E
Come a little closer, baby,

Asus2 E Asus2
I feel like lettin' go

E Asus2
Of ev'ry - thing that stands between ___ us

E Asus2
And the love we used to know.

C♯m A
I wanna touch you like a cleansing rain

C♯m A
And let it wash all the hurt away.

E
So, come a little closer, baby,

Asus2 E
I feel like lettin' go.

Bridge

A
If there's still a chance, then take my hand

E Esus4 E
And we'll steal away

A
Off in - to the night till we make things right.

F♯m11 B
The sun's gonna rise on a better day.

Guitar Solo

‖: E | A | E | A :‖

Verse 3

```
E
   Come a little closer, baby,
Asus2                    E       Asus2
   I feel like strippin' it down.
E                        Asus2
   Back to the basics of you and me
                             E               Asus2
And what makes the world ___ go 'round.
C#m                     A
   Ev'ry inch of you a - gainst my skin.
C#m                                A
   I wanna be stronger than we've ___ ever been.
E
   So, come a little closer, baby,
Asus2                    E       Asus2
   I feel like strippin' it down.
E                             Asus2
    Come a little closer, baby,
E                           Asus2
   Just a little closer, baby.
E                             Asus2
   Come a little closer, baby,
                       E       Asus2
I feel like layin' you ___ down.
```

Outro

```
||: E      | A      | E      | A      :|| Repeat and fade
```

Country Girl
(Shake It for Me)

Words and Music by
Luke Bryan and Dallas Davidson

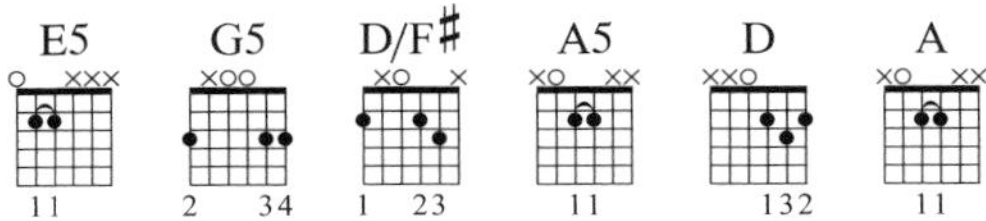

Intro	E5	G5	D/F#	E5
		G5	D/F#	E5

Verse 1

```
E5
Got a little boom in my big truck.
       G5
Gonna open up the doors and turn it up.
       D/F#
Gonna stomp my boots in the Georgia mud.
       E5
Gonna watch you make me fall in love.

Get up on the hood of my daddy's tractor,
G5
Up on the toolbox, it don't matter.
      D/F#
Down ___ on the tailgate, girl,
             E5
I can't wait to watch you do your thing.
```

```
                    E5
Pre-Chorus 1   Shake it for the young bucks sittin' in the honky-tonks,
                  G5
               For the rednecks rockin' till the break of dawn,
                  D/F#
               The D.J. spinnin' that country song.
                        E5
               Come on, ____ come on, come on.

               Shake it for the birds, shake it for the bees,
                                 G5
               Shake it for the catfish swimmin' down deep in the creek,
                         D/F#
               For the crickets and the critters and the squirrels.
                                   E5
               Shake it to the moon, shake it for me, girl.

               E5                            G5
Chorus 1       Country girl, shake it for me, ____ girl,
                                A5                            E5    D  A
               Shake it for me, ____ girl, shake it for me.
               E5                           G5
               Country girl, shake it for me, ____ girl,
                                A5                          E5
               Shake it for me, ____ girl, shake it for me.

               E5
Verse 2        Somebody's sweet little farmer's child
                   G5
               That got it in her blood to get a little wild,
               D/F#                                 E5
                  Ponytail and a pretty smile, rope ____ me in from a country mile.

               So, come on over here and get in my arms,
                    G5
               Spin ____ me around this big ol' barn,
               F#5                                E5
               Tangle me up like Grandma's yarn.    Yeah, yeah, yeah.
```

Pre-Chorus 2 *Repeat Pre-Chorus 1*

Chorus 2 *Repeat Chorus 1*

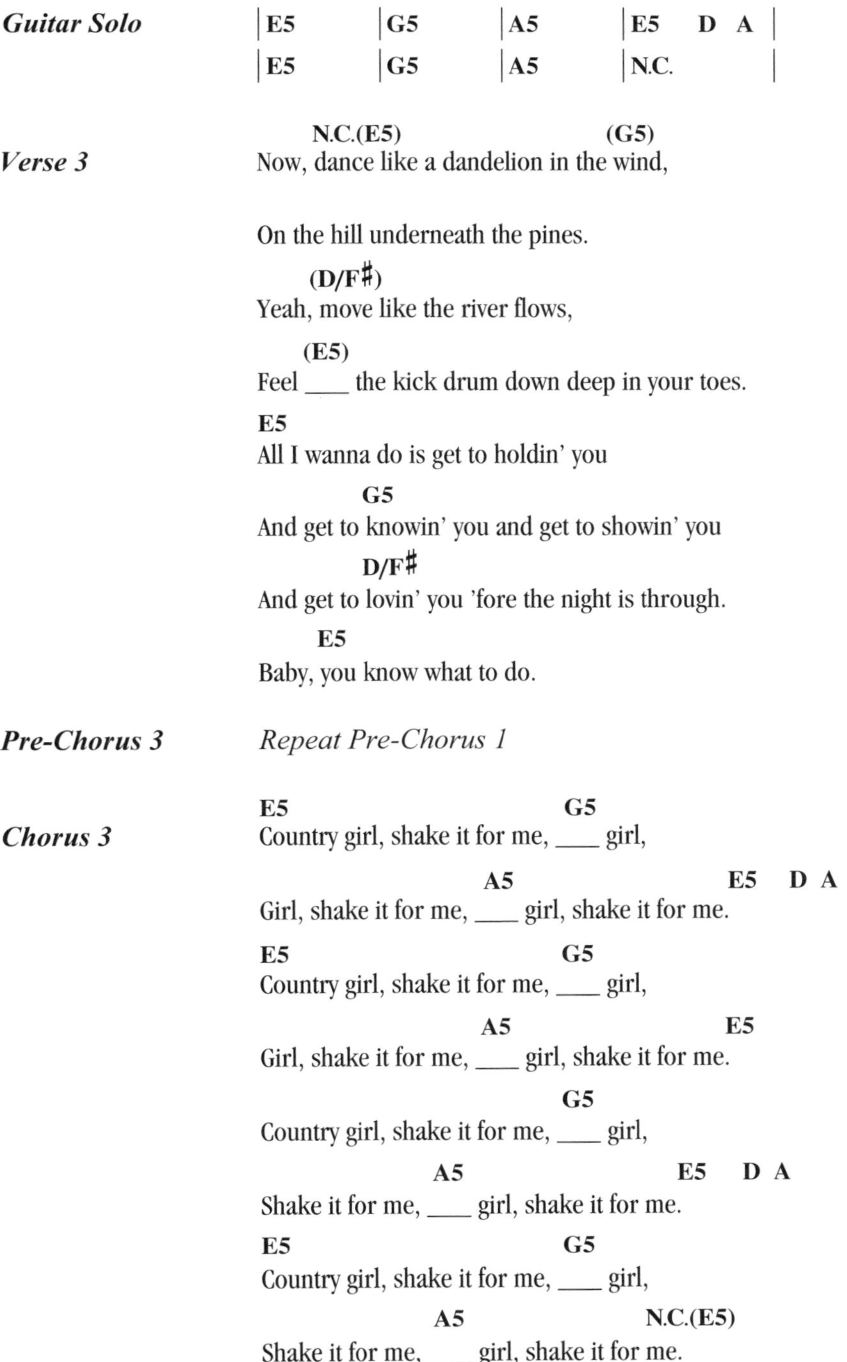

Guitar Solo

E5	G5	A5	E5 D A
E5	G5	A5	N.C.

Verse 3

N.C.(E5) (G5)
Now, dance like a dandelion in the wind,

On the hill underneath the pines.

(D/F♯)
Yeah, move like the river flows,

(E5)
Feel ___ the kick drum down deep in your toes.

E5
All I wanna do is get to holdin' you

G5
And get to knowin' you and get to showin' you

D/F♯
And get to lovin' you 'fore the night is through.

E5
Baby, you know what to do.

Pre-Chorus 3

Repeat Pre-Chorus 1

Chorus 3

E5 G5
Country girl, shake it for me, ___ girl,

A5 E5 D A
Girl, shake it for me, ___ girl, shake it for me.

E5 G5
Country girl, shake it for me, ___ girl,

A5 E5
Girl, shake it for me, ___ girl, shake it for me.

G5
Country girl, shake it for me, ___ girl,

A5 E5 D A
Shake it for me, ___ girl, shake it for me.

E5 G5
Country girl, shake it for me, ___ girl,

A5 N.C.(E5)
Shake it for me, ___ girl, shake it for me.

Crash My Party

Words and Music by
Ashley Gorley and Rodney Clawson

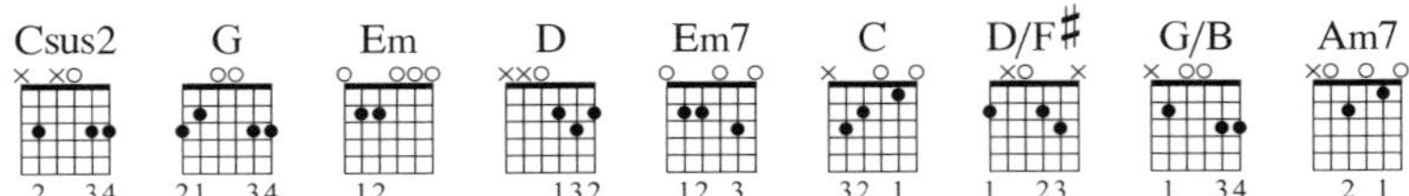

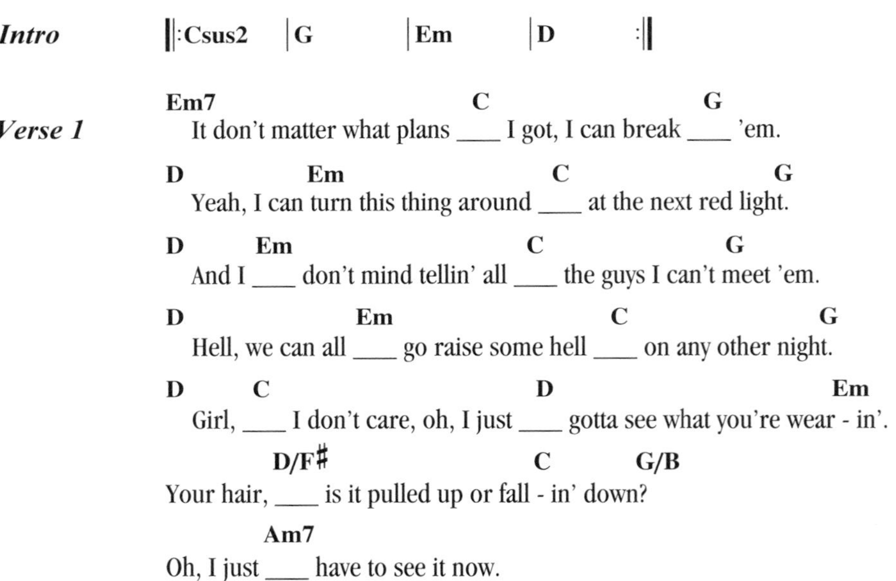

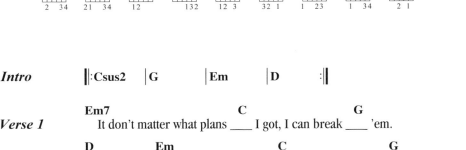

Intro ‖: Csus2 | G | Em | D :‖

Verse 1

```
Em7                        C                  G
  It don't matter what plans ___ I got, I can break ___ 'em.
D            Em                     C                 G
  Yeah, I can turn this thing around ___ at the next red light.
D         Em                       C                G
  And I ___ don't mind tellin' all ___ the guys I can't meet 'em.
D                  Em                     C                G
  Hell, we can all ___ go raise some hell ___ on any other night.
D       C                       D                          Em
  Girl, ___ I don't care, oh, I just ___ gotta see what you're wear - in'.
              D/F♯                  C       G/B
Your hair, ___ is it pulled up or fall - in' down?
             Am7
Oh, I just ___ have to see it now.
```

```
           N.C.          C                     G
Chorus 1   If you wanna call me, call me, call me,

                             Em7                 D
           You don't have to worry 'bout it, ba - by.

                               C                      G
           You can wake me up ___ in the dead of the night.

                             Em                   D
           Wreck my plans, ___ baby, that's alright.

               G/B        C              G
           This is a drop ___ ev'rything ___ kinda thing.

           Em                   D
           Swing on by, I'll pour ___ you a drink.

                         C                   G
           The door's ___ unlocked. I'll leave ___ on the lights.

                Em                     D         Csus2  G  Em
           Baby, you can crash my par - ty anytime.

           D            Em                       C                    G
Verse 2      Ain't a spot ___ downtown that's rock - in' the way that you rock __ me.

           D           Em                            C                G
             Ain't a bar ___ that can make me buzz ___ the way that you do.

           D                           Em                C
             I could be on the front ___ row of the best ___ show

                          G                           D
           And look down ___ and see your face on my ___ phone,

                          Em              C
           And I'm gone, ___ so long, hang ___ on.

                       D
           I'll meet ___ you in a minute or two.
```

Chorus 2

```
G/B          C                      G
If you wanna call me, call me, call me,

                   Em7                D
You don't have to worry 'bout it, ba - by.

                        C                        G
You can wake me up ___ in the dead of the night.

                  Em                    D
Wreck my plans, ___ baby, that's alright.

     G/B         C                G
This is a drop ___ ev'rything ___ kinda thing.

Em                          D
Swing on by, I'll pour ___ you a drink.

              C                         G
The door's ___ unlocked. I'll leave ___ on the lights.

      Em                       D
Baby, you can crash my par - ty anytime.
```

Guitar Solo

```
| C        | G        | Em       | D        |
| C        | G        | Em       | D        |
```

Bridge

```
               Csus2                          D
If it's two ___ in the mornin' and you're ___ feelin' lonely

              Em                   D
And won - derin' what I'm do - in'...
```

Chorus 3

```
                C                       G
Go ahead and call me, call me, call me.

                    Em7                 D
You don't have to worry 'bout it, ba - by.

                G/B     C                           G
You can wake me up ___ in the dead of the night.

                    Em                      D
Wreck my plans, ___ baby, that's alright.

                        C               G
And this is a drop ___ ev'rything ___ kinda thing.

Em                          D
Swing on by, I'll pour ___ you a drink.

                C                       G
The door's ___ unlocked. I'll leave ___ on the lights.

      Em                        D           C   G   Em7   D
Baby, you can crash my par - ty anytime.

C  G        Em7                     D           Csus2
       Baby, you can crash my par - ty anytime.
```

Outro

```
||: Csus2  |          |          |          :||
```

Cruise

Words and Music by Chase Rice,
Tyler Hubbard, Brian Kelley,
Joey Moi and Jesse Rice

(Capo 1st fret)

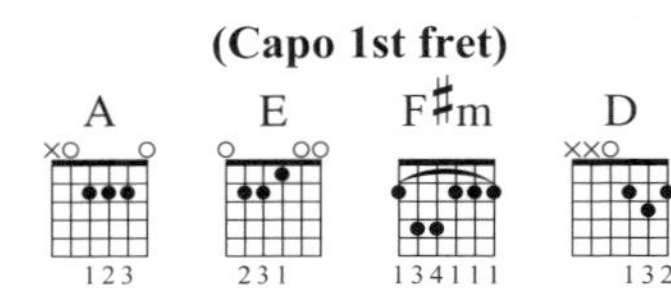

Chorus 1

```
A                         E
Baby, you a song, you make me wanna
         F♯m                D
Roll my windows down and cruise.
‖: A        | E        | F♯m       | D        :‖
```

Verse 1

```
             A                   E
Yeah, when I first saw that biki - ni top on her,
      F♯m                      D
She's poppin' right outta the South ___ Georgia water,
                A                           E
Thought, "Oh, ___ good Lord, she had them long tanned legs."
         F♯m            D
Couldn't    help myself, so I walked up and said:
```

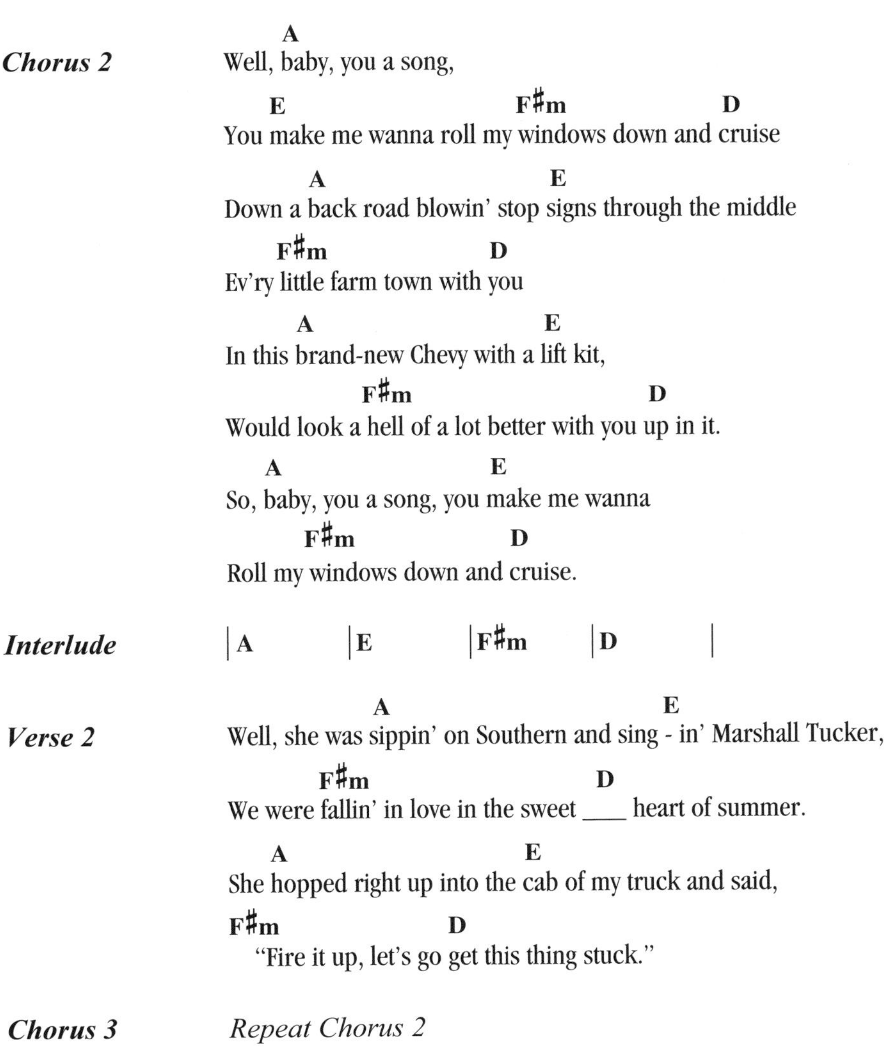

Chorus 2

A
Well, baby, you a song,
E F♯m D
You make me wanna roll my windows down and cruise
A E
Down a back road blowin' stop signs through the middle
F♯m D
Ev'ry little farm town with you
A E
In this brand-new Chevy with a lift kit,
F♯m D
Would look a hell of a lot better with you up in it.
A E
So, baby, you a song, you make me wanna
F♯m D
Roll my windows down and cruise.

Interlude

| A | E | F♯m | D |

Verse 2

A E
Well, she was sippin' on Southern and sing - in' Marshall Tucker,
F♯m D
We were fallin' in love in the sweet ___ heart of summer.
A E
She hopped right up into the cab of my truck and said,
F♯m D
"Fire it up, let's go get this thing stuck."

Chorus 3

Repeat Chorus 2

```
Guitar Solo     ‖: A      | E      | F#m      | D      :‖

                      A                    E
Verse 3         When that ___ summer sun fell ___ to his knees,
                 F#m                     D
                I ___ looked at her and she ___ looked at me
                     A               E
                And I    turned on those K.C. lights
                          F#m                   D
                And drove ___ all night 'cause it felt so right.

                Her and I, man, we felt so right.

                 A                        E
Verse 4         I put it in park and grabbed ___ my guitar
                              F#m                           D
                And strummed ___ a couple chords and sang ___ from the heart.
                A                E
                Girl, you sure got the beat in my chest bumpin'.
                F#m                D
                  Hell, I can't get you outta my head.

                A
Chorus 4        Baby, you a song,
                   E                       F#m                D
                You make me wanna roll my windows down and cruise
                       A                      E
                Down a back road blowin' stop signs through the middle
                   F#m                D
                Ev'ry little farm town with you.
```

Chorus 5

```
         A
Well, baby, you a song,
      E                                F#m                D
You make me wanna roll my windows down and cruise
          A                           E
Down a back road blowin'stop signs through the middle
       F#m                  D
Ev'ry little farm town with you
        A                             E
In this brand-new Chevy with a lift kit,
                 F#m                               D
Would look a hell of a lot better with you up in it.
            A
Come on, baby, you a song,
      E                                F#m                D
You make me wanna roll my windows down and cruise.
A   E
        Come on, girl.
F#m         D                         A    E  F#m  D
   Get those windows down and cruise.
         A
Ah, yeah.
```

Don't You Wanna Stay

Words and Music by Jason Sellers,
Paul Jenkins and Andrew Gibson

Melody:

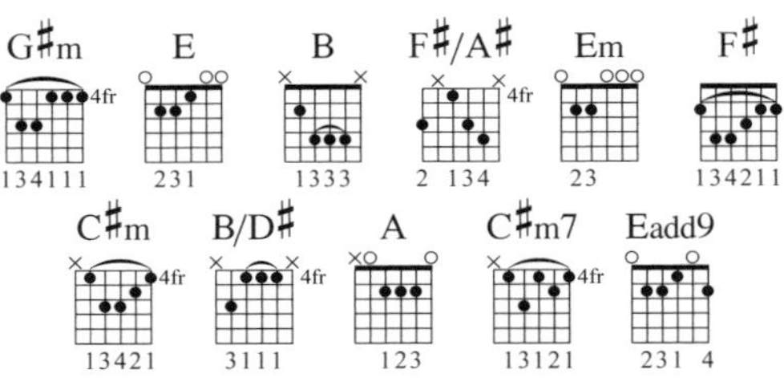

Intro ‖: **G♯m** | **E** | **B** | **F♯/A♯** :‖

Verse 1

G♯m **E** **B** **F♯/A♯**
Male: I really hate to let ___ this moment go,

G♯m **E** **B**
Touchin' your skin and your ___ hair fallin' slow,

E **Em**
When a goodbye kiss feels like this.

Chorus 1

B **G♯m** **F♯**
Both: Don't you wanna stay here a little while?

C♯m
Don't you wanna hold each other tight?

B/D♯ **E** **F♯**
Don't you wanna fall asleep with me tonight?

B **G♯m** **E** **F♯**
Don't you wanna stay here a little while?

C♯m **B/D♯**
We can make for - ever feel this way.

E **G♯m** **E** **B** **F♯/A♯** **G♯m** **E** **B** **F♯/A♯**
Don't you wanna stay?

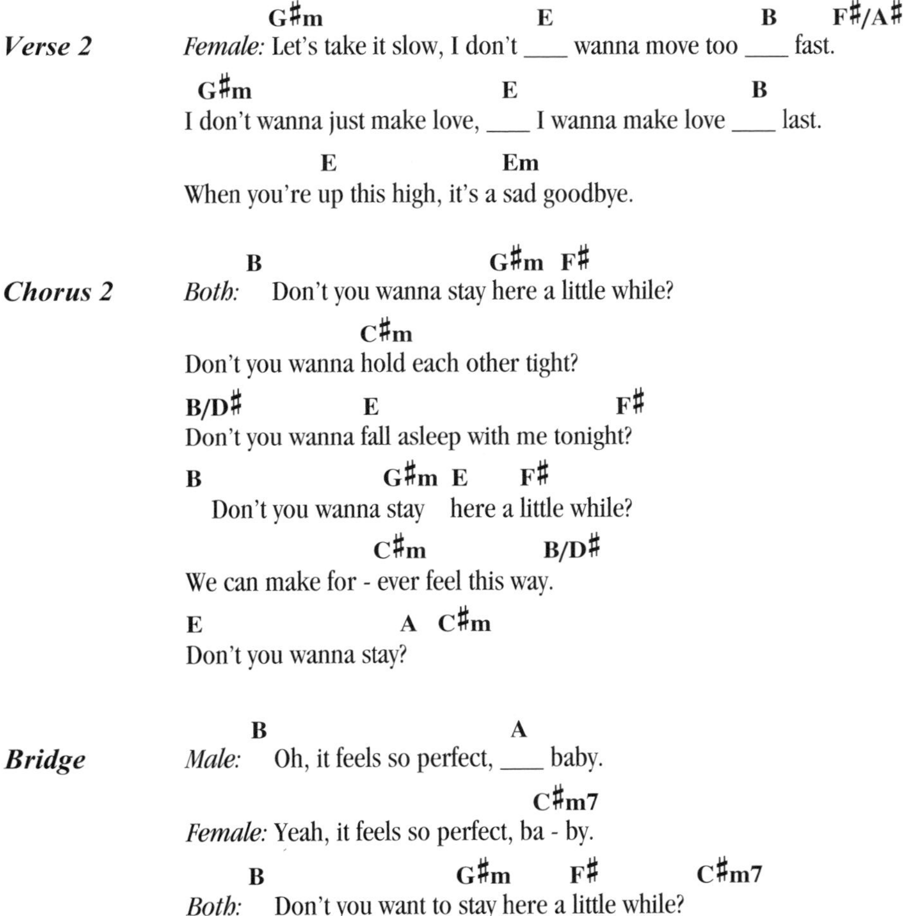

Verse 2

G♯m E B F♯/A♯
Female: Let's take it slow, I don't ___ wanna move too ___ fast.

G♯m E B
I don't wanna just make love, ___ I wanna make love ___ last.

E Em
When you're up this high, it's a sad goodbye.

Chorus 2

B G♯m F♯
Both: Don't you wanna stay here a little while?

C♯m
Don't you wanna hold each other tight?

B/D♯ E F♯
Don't you wanna fall asleep with me tonight?

B G♯m E F♯
Don't you wanna stay here a little while?

C♯m B/D♯
We can make for - ever feel this way.

E A C♯m
Don't you wanna stay?

Bridge

B A
Male: Oh, it feels so perfect, ___ baby.

C♯m7
Female: Yeah, it feels so perfect, ba - by.

B G♯m F♯ C♯m7
Both: Don't you want to stay here a little while?

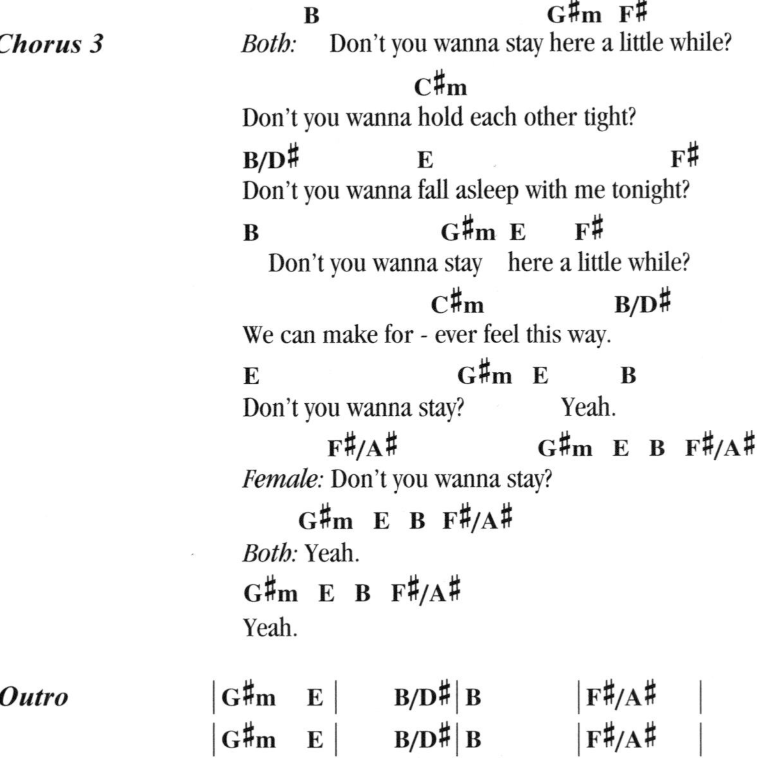

Chorus 3

B G♯m F♯
Both: Don't you wanna stay here a little while?

C♯m
Don't you wanna hold each other tight?

B/D♯ E F♯
Don't you wanna fall asleep with me tonight?

B G♯m E F♯
Don't you wanna stay here a little while?

C♯m B/D♯
We can make for - ever feel this way.

E G♯m E B
Don't you wanna stay? Yeah.

F♯/A♯ G♯m E B F♯/A♯
Female: Don't you wanna stay?

G♯m E B F♯/A♯
Both: Yeah.

G♯m E B F♯/A♯
Yeah.

Outro

| G♯m E | B/D♯ | B | F♯/A♯ |
| G♯m E | B/D♯ | B | F♯/A♯ |
| G♯m E | Eadd9 | | ‖

Farmer's Daughter

Words and Music by Rhett Akins,
Ben Hayslip and Marv Green

Tune down 1/2 step:
(low to high) E♭-A♭-D♭-G♭-B♭-E♭

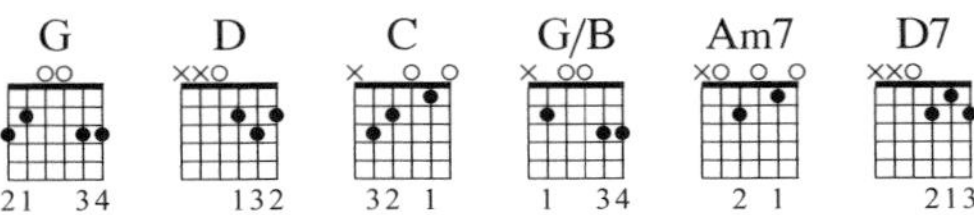

Intro ‖: G | | D | :‖

Verse 1

```
         G
Well, I heard he needed some help on the farm.
         D                    G
Some - body with a truck and two strong arms,
                         D
Not scared of dirt and willin' to work
         C    G/B      Am7  D
Till the sun goes down.
     G                        C
So, I pulled up and said, "I'm ___ your man.
     D7                      G
I can start right now." And we ___ shook hands.
                                        D7
He said, "The fence needs fixin', the peaches need pickin'
          C
And the cows need bringin' 'round."
```

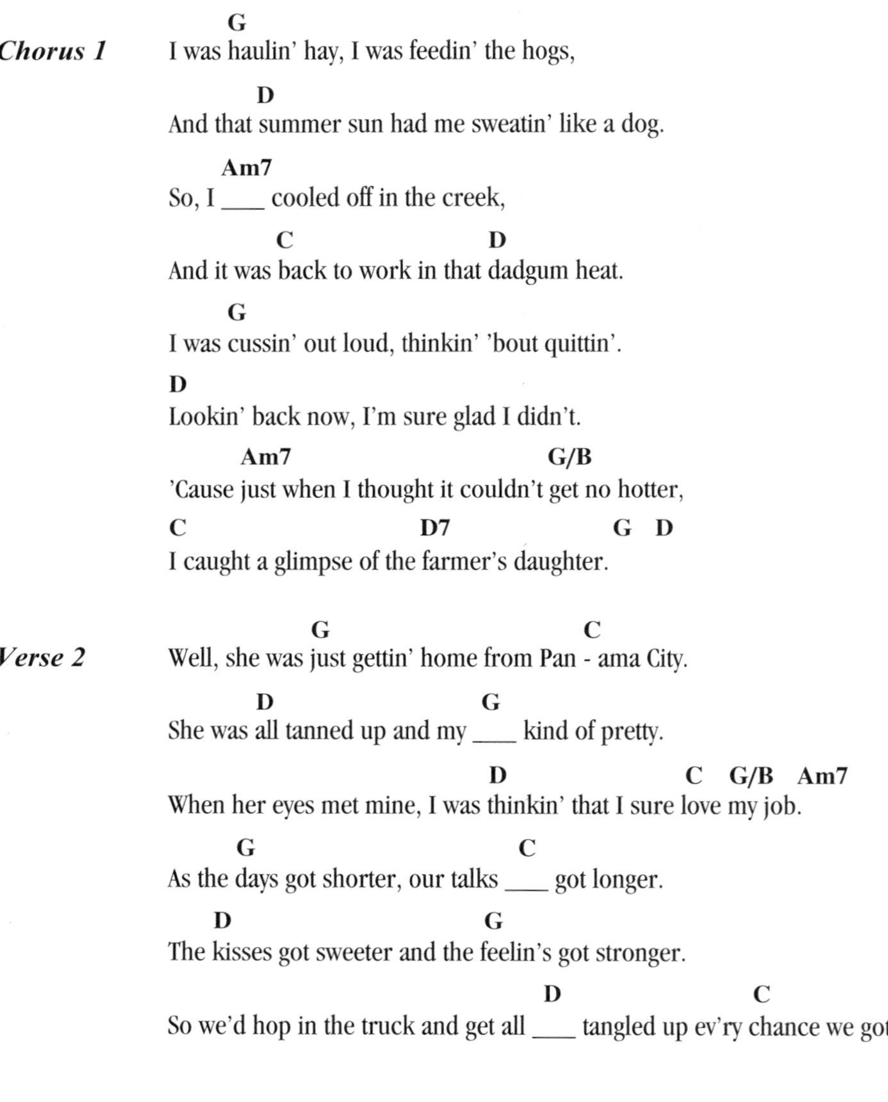

Chorus 1

G
I was haulin' hay, I was feedin' the hogs,

D
And that summer sun had me sweatin' like a dog.

Am7
So, I ___ cooled off in the creek,

C   **D**
And it was back to work in that dadgum heat.

G
I was cussin' out loud, thinkin' 'bout quittin'.

D
Lookin' back now, I'm sure glad I didn't.

Am7   **G/B**
'Cause just when I thought it couldn't get no hotter,

C   **D7**   **G**   **D**
I caught a glimpse of the farmer's daughter.

Verse 2

G   **C**
Well, she was just gettin' home from Pan - ama City.

D   **G**
She was all tanned up and my ___ kind of pretty.

D   **C**   **G/B**   **Am7**
When her eyes met mine, I was thinkin' that I sure love my job.

G   **C**
As the days got shorter, our talks ___ got longer.

D   **G**
The kisses got sweeter and the feelin's got stronger.

D   **C**
So we'd hop in the truck and get all ___ tangled up ev'ry chance we got.

```
                 G
Chorus 2         We were down by the river all night long.
                      D
                 When the sun came up, I was sneakin' her home,
                    Am7
                 And draggin' my butt to work
                        C                          D
                 With the smell of her perfume on my shirt.
                    G
                 I be on the tractor, she'd be on my mind
                       D
                 With that sun beatin' down on this back of mine.
                    Am7                               G/B
                 And just when I thought it couldn't get no hotter,
                 C                        D7
                 I fell in love with the farmer's daughter.

                 Am7                      D
Bridge             We got married last ___ spring.
                      Am7                                  D
                 Whoa, ___ and there ain't no better life for me.

                       G
Chorus 3         I'm still haulin' hay and feedin' the hogs
                      D
                 And that summer sun's got me sweatin' like a dog.
                      Am7
                 So, I ___ cool off in the creek,
                       C                              D
                 And she brings me out a glass of sweet iced tea.
                       G
                 Now I'm on the tractor, she's on my mind.
                    D
                 And I can't wait till it's quittin' time.
                    Am7                      G/B
                 And just what I think it can't get no hotter,
                 C                    D7                      G     D
                 I come home to the farmer's daughter,
                                      G      D     G
                 The farmer's daugh - ter.
```

Follow Your Arrow

Words and Music by
Kacey Musgraves,
Shane McAnally
and Brandy Clark

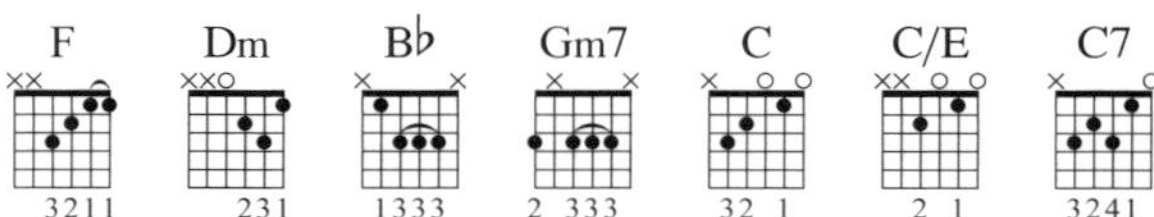

Intro | **F** | **Dm** | **F** | **Dm** |

Verse 1

```
          F
If you save yourself for marriage, you're a bore.
              Dm
If you don't save yourself for marriage, you're a horrible person.
 B♭
If you won't have a drink, then you're a prude.
            Gm7                      C
But they'll call you a drunk as soon as you down the first one.
 F
If you can't lose the weight, then you're just fat.
   Dm
But if you lose too much, then you're on crack.
         B♭
You're damned if you do and you're damned if you don't.
        Gm7                     C
So, you might as well just do what - ever you want.
```

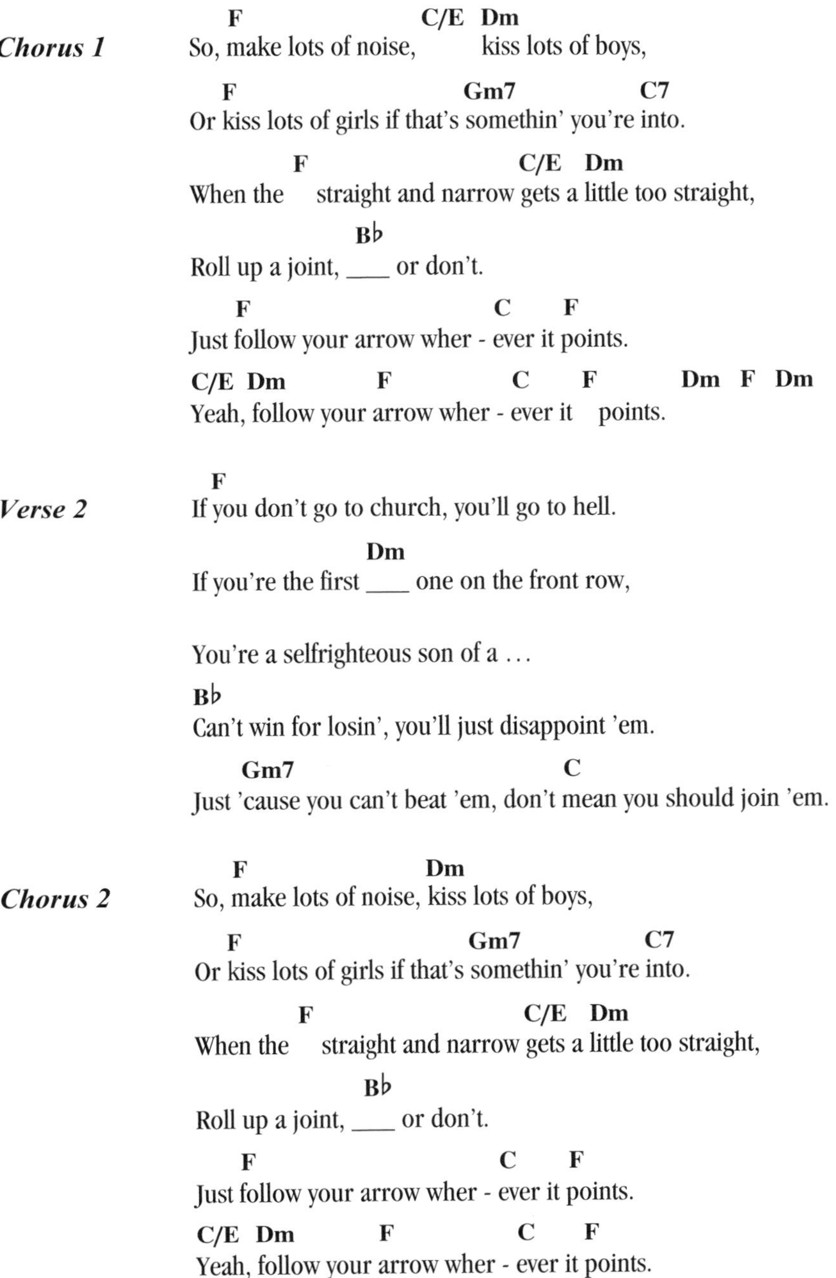

Chorus 1

F C/E Dm
So, make lots of noise, kiss lots of boys,

F Gm7 C7
Or kiss lots of girls if that's somethin' you're into.

F C/E Dm
When the straight and narrow gets a little too straight,

B♭
Roll up a joint, ___ or don't.

F C F
Just follow your arrow wher - ever it points.

C/E Dm F C F Dm F Dm
Yeah, follow your arrow wher - ever it points.

Verse 2

F
If you don't go to church, you'll go to hell.

Dm
If you're the first ___ one on the front row,

You're a selfrighteous son of a …

B♭
Can't win for losin', you'll just disappoint 'em.

Gm7 C
Just 'cause you can't beat 'em, don't mean you should join 'em.

Chorus 2

F Dm
So, make lots of noise, kiss lots of boys,

F Gm7 C7
Or kiss lots of girls if that's somethin' you're into.

F C/E Dm
When the straight and narrow gets a little too straight,

B♭
Roll up a joint, ___ or don't.

F C F
Just follow your arrow wher - ever it points.

C/E Dm F C F
Yeah, follow your arrow wher - ever it points.

```
                F                    Dm
Bridge          Say what you think, love who you love,

                       F                     Dm
                'Cause you just get so many trips 'round the sun.

                          B♭   Gm7    F      Dm  F  Dm
                Yeah, you only, only live once.


                    F                 Dm
Chorus 3        So, make lots of noise, kiss lots of boys,

                   F                Gm7              C7
                Or kiss lots of girls if that's what you're into.

                          F                           Dm
                When the  straight and narrow gets a little too straight,

                                Bb
                Roll up a joint, ___ I would.

                    F                        C     F
                And follow your arrow wher - ever it points.

                C/E  Dm       F             C     F      Dm  F  Dm  C  F
                Yeah, follow your arrow wher - ever it points.
```

God Gave Me You

Words and Music by
Dave Barnes

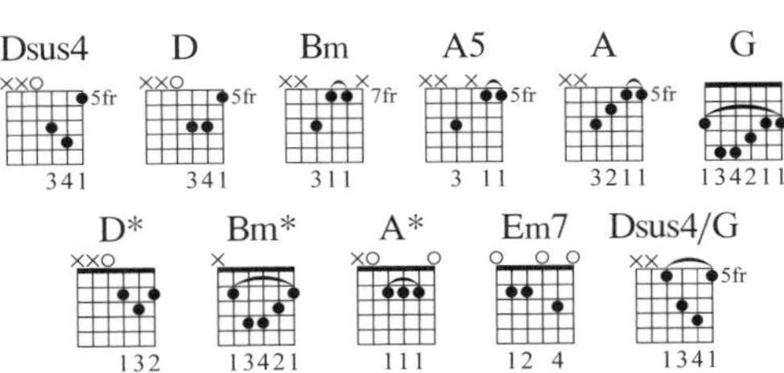

Intro | Dsus4 D | Bm A5 | Dsus4 D | Bm A |

Verse 1

```
G              D*
  I've been ___ a walking heartache,
Bm*            A*
  I've made ___ a mess of me.
G                D*
  The person ___ that I've been lately
Bm*             A*
  Ain't who ___ I wanna be.
     G                 D*
But,   you stay here ___ right beside me
Bm                A*
  And watch as ___ the storm blows through.
    Em7        G
And I need you.
```

```
                  G                   D*                    Bm*  A*
Chorus 1    'Cause God ___ gave me you for the ups and downs.

               G                D*               Bm*  A*
            God ___ gave me you for the days of doubt.

                             G          D*
            For when I think ___ I've lost my way,

                                Bm*          A*
            There are no words ___ here left to say.

                      Em7  G     A*         G  D*  Bm*  A*
            It's true, ___     God gave me you.

                        G  D* Bm* A*
            Gave me you.

            G                        D*
Verse 2        There's more here ___ than what we're seeing,

            Bm*         A*
               A divine ___ conspiracy,

            G             D*
               That you, ___ an angel lovely,

            Bm*              A*
               Could some - how fall for me.

            G                 D*
               You'll always ___ be love's great martyr,

            Bm*              A*
               And I'll be ___ the flattered fool.

               Em7          G
            And I need you. ___ Yeah.
```

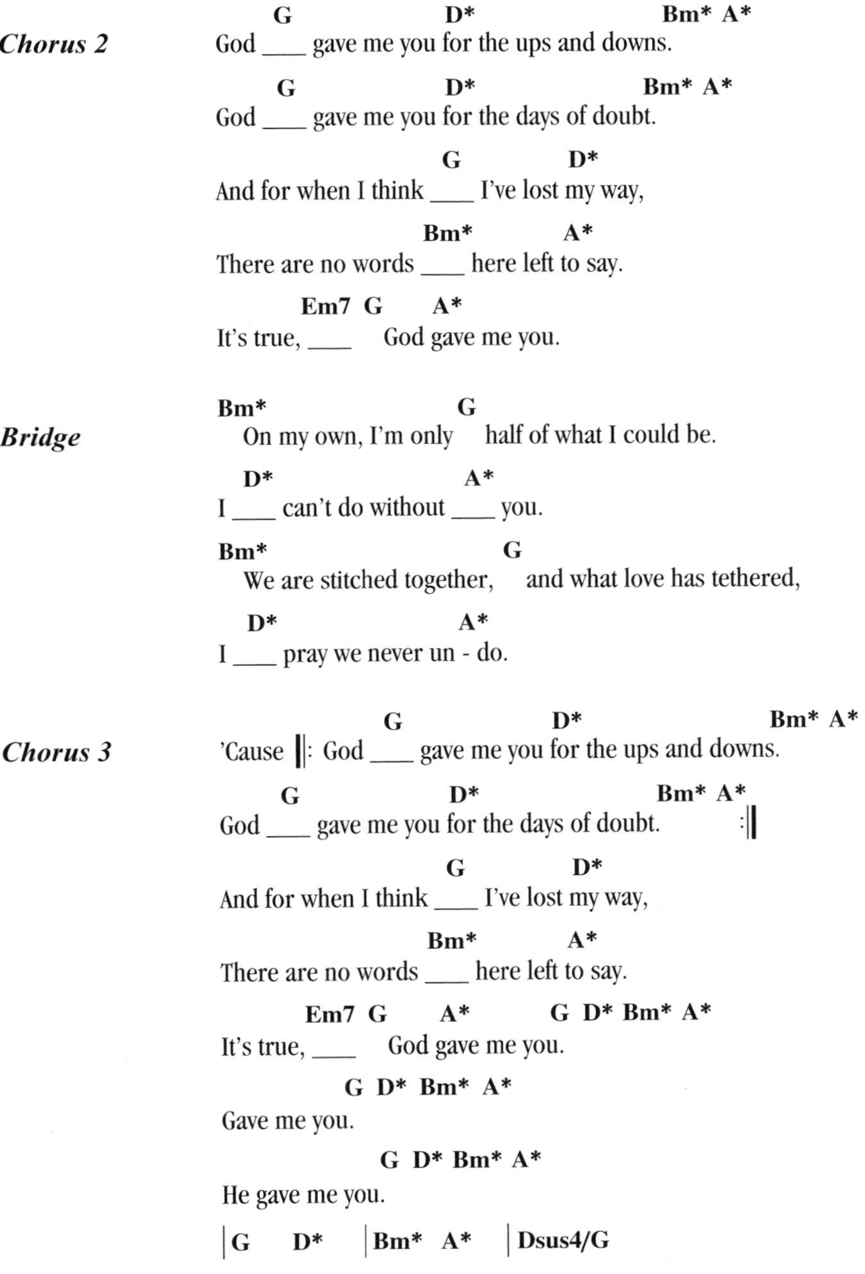

Chorus 2

G D* Bm* A*
God ___ gave me you for the ups and downs.

G D* Bm* A*
God ___ gave me you for the days of doubt.

G D*
And for when I think ___ I've lost my way,

Bm* A*
There are no words ___ here left to say.

Em7 G A*
It's true, ___ God gave me you.

Bridge

Bm* G
On my own, I'm only half of what I could be.

D* A*
I ___ can't do without ___ you.

Bm* G
We are stitched together, and what love has tethered,

D* A*
I ___ pray we never un - do.

Chorus 3

G D* Bm* A*
'Cause ‖: God ___ gave me you for the ups and downs.

G D* Bm* A*
God ___ gave me you for the days of doubt. :‖

G D*
And for when I think ___ I've lost my way,

Bm* A*
There are no words ___ here left to say.

Em7 G A* G D* Bm* A*
It's true, ___ God gave me you.

G D* Bm* A*
Gave me you.

G D* Bm* A*
He gave me you.

| G D* | Bm* A* | Dsus4/G

The Good Stuff

Words and Music by
Craig Wiseman and Jim Collins

Melody:
Well, me and my la - dy had our

G (21 34) D/F♯ (T 132) Em (12) G/D (4) C (32 1) G/B (1 34)
Am7 (2 1) Dsus4 (134) D (132) G7 (131211) Em7 (12 3)

Intro

| N.C. | G | D/F♯ | |
| Em | G/D | C | | |

Verse 1

```
      G                    D/F♯
Well, me and my lady had our first big fight,
    Em                        G/D          C
So I drove around till I saw the neon lights of a corner bar
     G/B                     Am7
And it just seemed just right, so I pulled up.
     G                   D/F♯
Not a soul around but the old ___ barkeep
      Em                    G/D
Down ___ at the end and lookin' half-asleep.
   C                   G/B                     Am7
But he walked up and said, "What'll it be?" I said, "The good stuff."
G/B  C                       Dsus4   D
   He didn't reach around for the whiskey,
   C              Dsus4  D
He didn't pour me a beer.
   C                     Dsus4   D
His blue eyes kinda went misty,
         Em
He said, "You can't find that here.
```

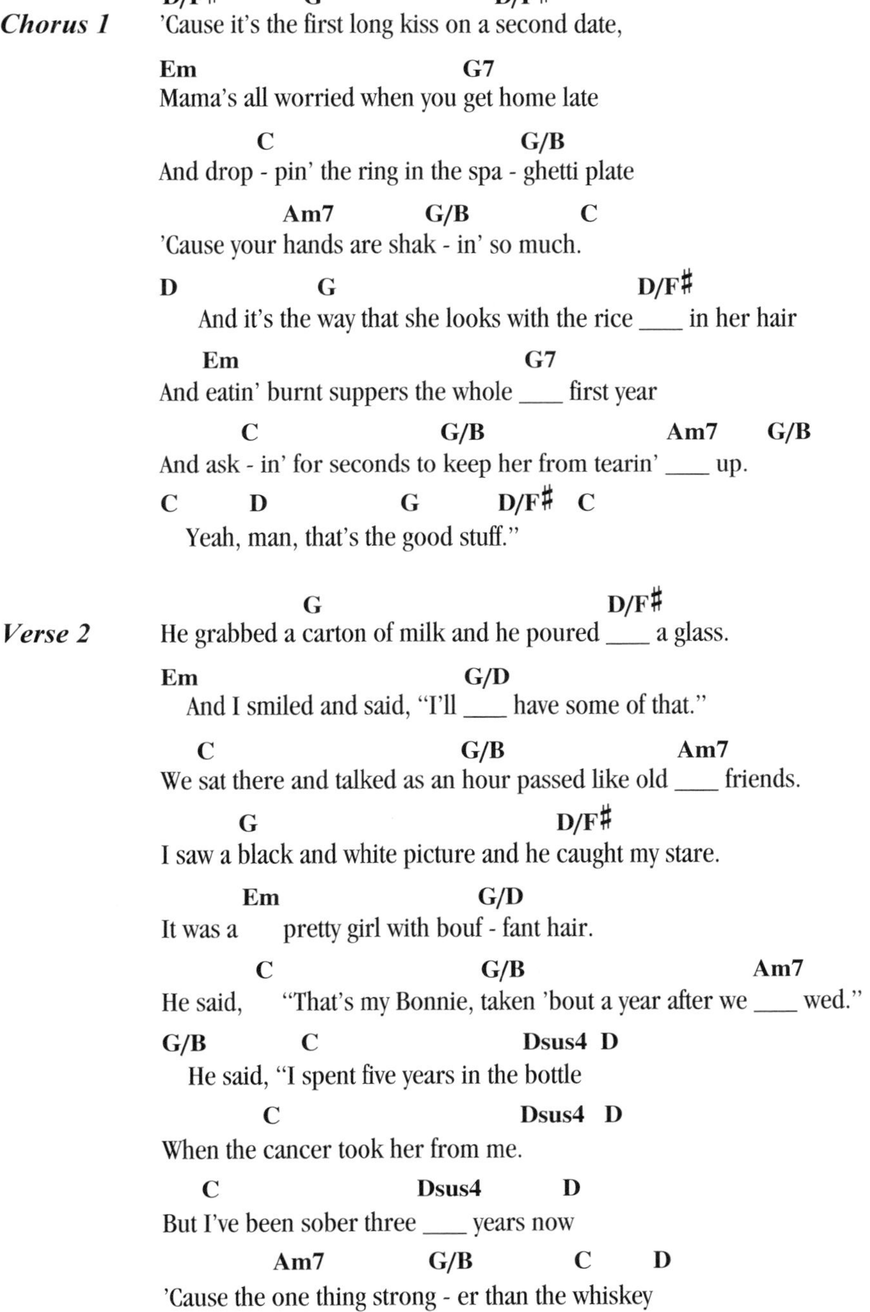

```
              D/F#        G                  D/F#
*Chorus 1*    'Cause it's the first long kiss on a second date,

              Em                          G7
              Mama's all worried when you get home late

                    C                           G/B
              And drop - pin' the ring in the spa - ghetti plate

                       Am7        G/B          C
              'Cause your hands are shak - in' so much.

              D            G                            D/F#
                And it's the way that she looks with the rice ___ in her hair

                 Em                           G7
              And eatin' burnt suppers the whole ___ first year

                   C                 G/B                   Am7     G/B
              And ask - in' for seconds to keep her from tearin' ___ up.

              C      D          G       D/F#  C
                Yeah, man, that's the good stuff."


                         G                         D/F#
*Verse 2*     He grabbed a carton of milk and he poured ___ a glass.

              Em                      G/D
                And I smiled and said, "I'll ___ have some of that."

                 C                     G/B                Am7
              We sat there and talked as an hour passed like old ___ friends.

                    G                         D/F#
              I saw a black and white picture and he caught my stare.

                    Em                  G/D
              It was a     pretty girl with bouf - fant hair.

                     C                 G/B                     Am7
              He said,     "That's my Bonnie, taken 'bout a year after we ___ wed."

              G/B         C                 Dsus4 D
                He said, "I spent five years in the bottle

                     C                      Dsus4  D
              When the cancer took her from me.

                 C                 Dsus4        D
              But I've been sober three ___ years now

                       Am7        G/B         C      D
              'Cause the one thing strong - er than the whiskey
```

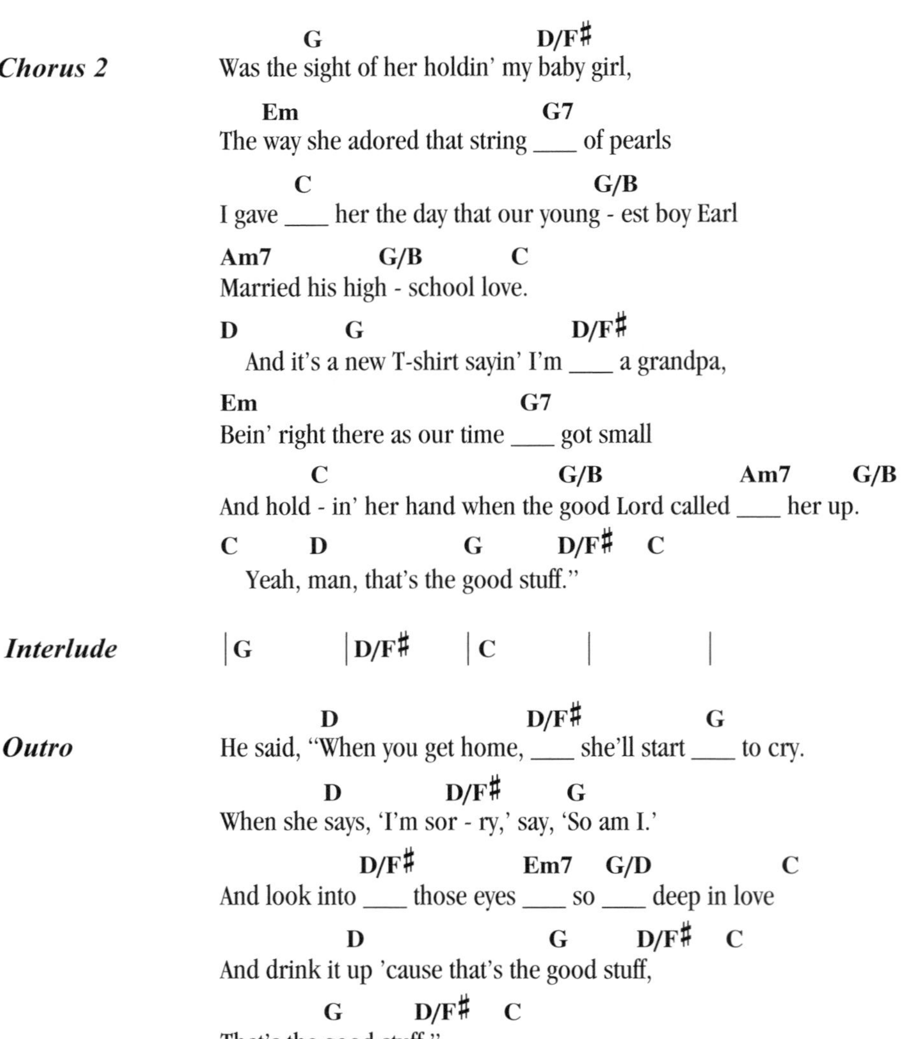

Chorus 2

G D/F#
Was the sight of her holdin' my baby girl,

Em G7
The way she adored that string ___ of pearls

C G/B
I gave ___ her the day that our young - est boy Earl

Am7 G/B C
Married his high - school love.

D G D/F#
And it's a new T-shirt sayin' I'm ___ a grandpa,

Em G7
Bein' right there as our time ___ got small

C G/B Am7 G/B
And hold - in' her hand when the good Lord called ___ her up.

C D G D/F# C
Yeah, man, that's the good stuff."

Interlude

| G | D/F# | C | | |

Outro

D D/F# G
He said, "When you get home, ___ she'll start ___ to cry.

D D/F# G
When she says, 'I'm sor - ry,' say, 'So am I.'

D/F# Em7 G/D C
And look into ___ those eyes ___ so ___ deep in love

D G D/F# C
And drink it up 'cause that's the good stuff,

G D/F# C
That's the good stuff."

Honey Bee

Words and Music by
Rhett Akins and Ben Hayslip

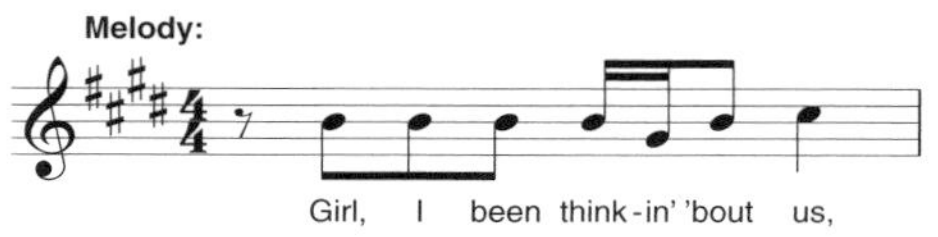

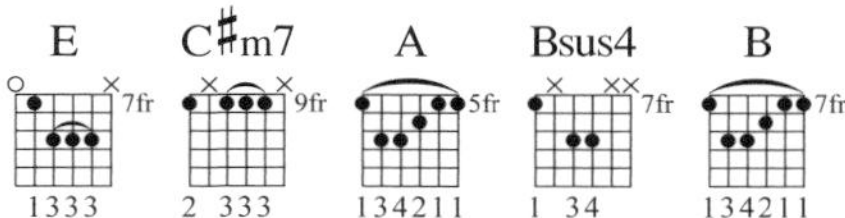

Intro ‖: E | C♯m7 | A | Bsus4 :‖

Verse 1

```
E                                  B
  Girl, I been thinkin' 'bout us,    and you know I ain't good at this stuff.
A
  But these feelin's pilin' up won't give me no rest.
E                                      B
  This might come out a little crazy,    a little sideways, yeah, maybe.
A
  I don't know how long it'll take me, but I'll do my best.
```

Chorus 1

```
E                             C♯m7                          A
  You'll be my soft and sweet,    I'll be your strong and steady.
                          B                          E
You'll be my glass of wine,   I'll be your shot of whiskey.
                       C♯m7
You'll be my sunny day,    I'll be your shade tree.
A                              B                       E  C♯m7  A  Bsus4
  You'll be my honeysuckle,      I'll be your honeybee.
```

Verse 2

```
E
   Yeah, that came out a little country,
B
   But ev'ry word was right on the money.
A
   And I got you smilin', honey, right back at me.
E
   Now hold on 'cause I ain't done.
B
   There's more where that came from.
A
   Well, you know I'm just havin' fun, but seriously.
```

Chorus 2

```
E                         C#m7
   You'll be my Louisiana,    I'll be your Mississippi.
A                             B
   You'll be my little Loretta,    I'll be your Conway Twitty.
E                             C#m7
   You'll be my sugar, baby,    I'll be your sweet iced tea.
A                             B
   You'll be my honeysuckle,    I'll be your honeybee.
```

Guitar Solo

```
||: E      | C#m7    | A       | B      :||
```

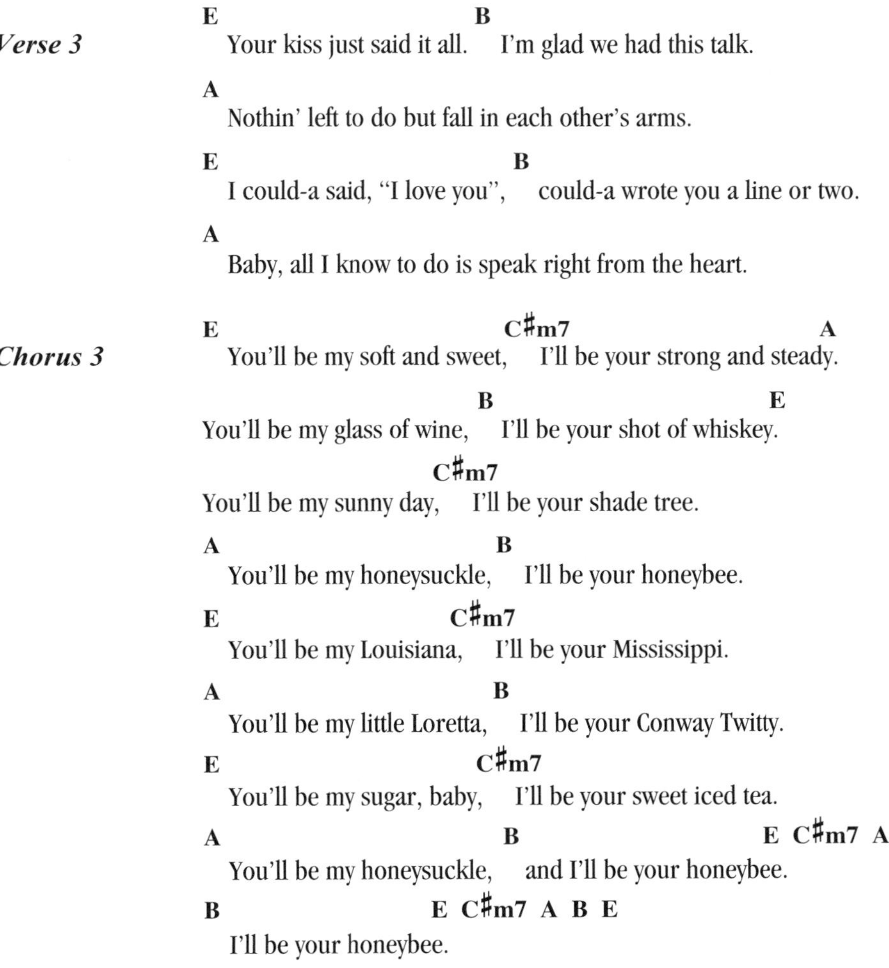

```
                E                         B
*Verse 3*         Your kiss just said it all.    I'm glad we had this talk.

                A
                  Nothin' left to do but fall in each other's arms.

                E                              B
                  I could-a said, "I love you",    could-a wrote you a line or two.

                A
                  Baby, all I know to do is speak right from the heart.

                E                              C#m7                       A
*Chorus 3*        You'll be my soft and sweet,     I'll be your strong and steady.

                                          B                         E
                You'll be my glass of wine,     I'll be your shot of whiskey.

                                    C#m7
                You'll be my sunny day,     I'll be your shade tree.

                A                          B
                  You'll be my honeysuckle,     I'll be your honeybee.

                E                    C#m7
                  You'll be my Louisiana,     I'll be your Mississippi.

                A                          B
                  You'll be my little Loretta,     I'll be your Conway Twitty.

                E                          C#m7
                  You'll be my sugar, baby,     I'll be your sweet iced tea.

                A                          B                         E  C#m7  A
                  You'll be my honeysuckle,     and I'll be your honeybee.

                B                    E  C#m7  A  B  E
                  I'll be your honeybee.
```

The House That Built Me

Words and Music by
Tom Douglas and Allen Shamblin

Drop D tuning:
(low to high) D-A-D-G-B-E

(Capo 3rd fret)

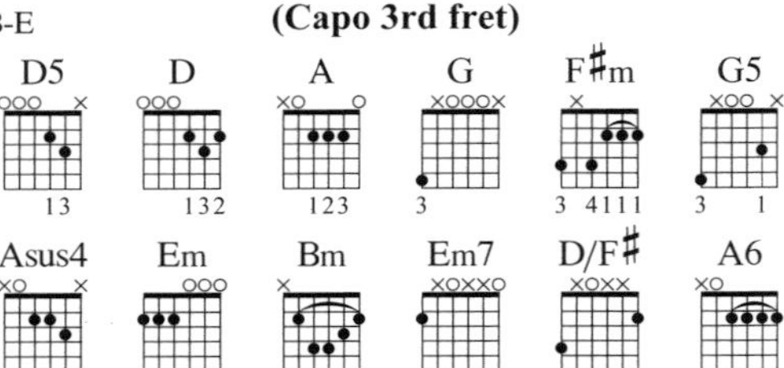

Intro

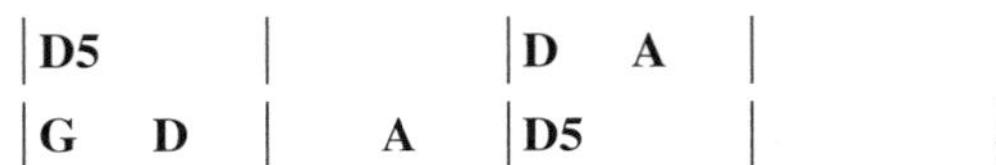

Verse 1

D5
I know they say ___ you can't go home again.
F♯m
I just had to come back one last time.
G5
Ma'am, I know you don't know me from Adam,
D5 **Asus4 A**
But these handprints on the front steps are mine.

Verse 2

D5
Up those stairs, __ in that little back bedroom,
F♯m
Is where I did my homework and I learned to play guitar.
G5
And I bet you didn't know, under that live oak,
D5 **Asus4 A**
My fav'rite dog is buried in the yard.

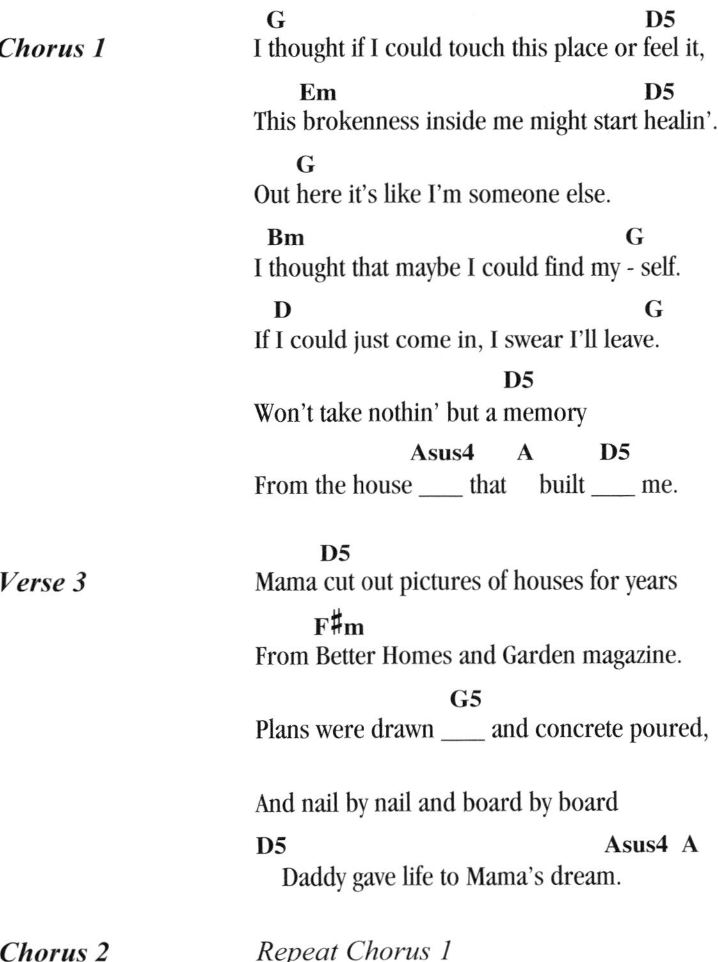

Chorus 1

G **D5**
I thought if I could touch this place or feel it,

Em **D5**
This brokenness inside me might start healin'.

G
Out here it's like I'm someone else.

Bm **G**
I thought that maybe I could find my - self.

D **G**
If I could just come in, I swear I'll leave.

D5
Won't take nothin' but a memory

Asus4 **A** **D5**
From the house ___ that built ___ me.

Verse 3

D5
Mama cut out pictures of houses for years

F♯m
From Better Homes and Garden magazine.

G5
Plans were drawn ___ and concrete poured,

And nail by nail and board by board

D5 **Asus4** **A**
Daddy gave life to Mama's dream.

Chorus 2

Repeat Chorus 1

Bridge

```
      Bm                                D5
You leave home, you move on and you do the best you can.

Em                                 G5        Asus4  A
I got lost in this old world and for - got who I am.
```

Chorus 3

```
   G                                  D5
I thought if I could touch this place or feel it,

     Em                               D5
This brokenness inside me might start healin'.

     G
Out here it's like I'm someone else.

  Bm                                 G
I thought that maybe I could find my - self.

   D5                  Em7        D/F#        G
If I could walk around, ___ I swear ___ I'll leave.

                                D5
Won't take nothin' but a memory

                  Asus4    A        G      D  Em  A6  D5
From the house ___ that   built ___ me.
```

I Drive Your Truck

Words and Music by
Connie Harrington,
Jimmy Yeary and
Jessica Alexander

Melody:

(Capo 2nd fret)

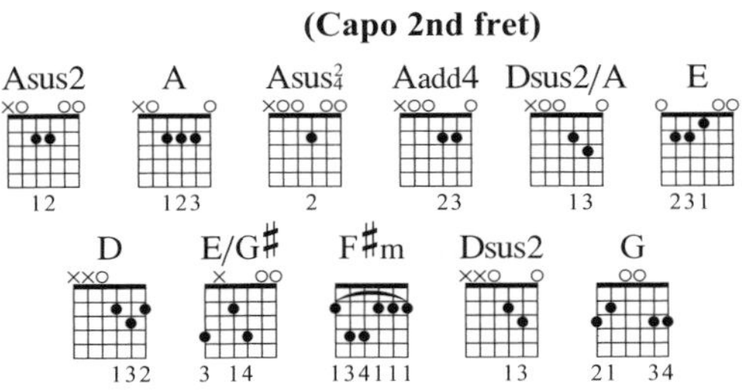

Intro ‖: **Asus2 A Asus2 | Asus$^{2}_{4}$ Aadd4 Asus$^{2}_{4}$** :‖

Verse 1

Asus2
Eight - y-nine cents in the ashtray,
Dsus2/A
Half empty bottle of Gatorade rollin' in the floor - board,

That dirty Braves cap on the dash.
Asus2
Dog ___ tags hangin' from the rearview,

Old Skoal can and cowboy boots
Dsus2/A
And a "Go Army" shirt folded in the back.
E **D**
This thing ___ burns gas like crazy but that's ___ alright.
E **D**
People got ___ their ways of copin', oh, and I ___ got mine.

Chorus 1

```
              A
I drive your truck.
        E/G♯                         F♯m
I roll ev - 'ry window down and I burn up
          D                   E
Ev'ry back ___ road in this town.
             A             E/G♯
I find a field. ___ I tear it up
              F♯m         E
Till all the pain's ___ a cloud of dust.
                D                         Asus2  A  Asus2
Yeah, sometimes ___ I drive your truck.
| Asus2/4   Aadd4   Asus2/4 |
```

Verse 2

```
 Asus2
I leave that radio playin'
                                              Dsus2
The same old country station where you left ___ it.

Yeah, man, I crank it up.
             Asus2
And you'd prob - 'ly punch my arm right now
                                          Dsus2
If you saw this tear rollin' down on my ___ face.

Hey, man, I'm tryin' to be tough.
       E
And Mom - ma asked me this mornin'
           D
If I'd been by ___ your grave.
          E                               D
But that flag ___ and stone ain't where I feel you an - yway.
```

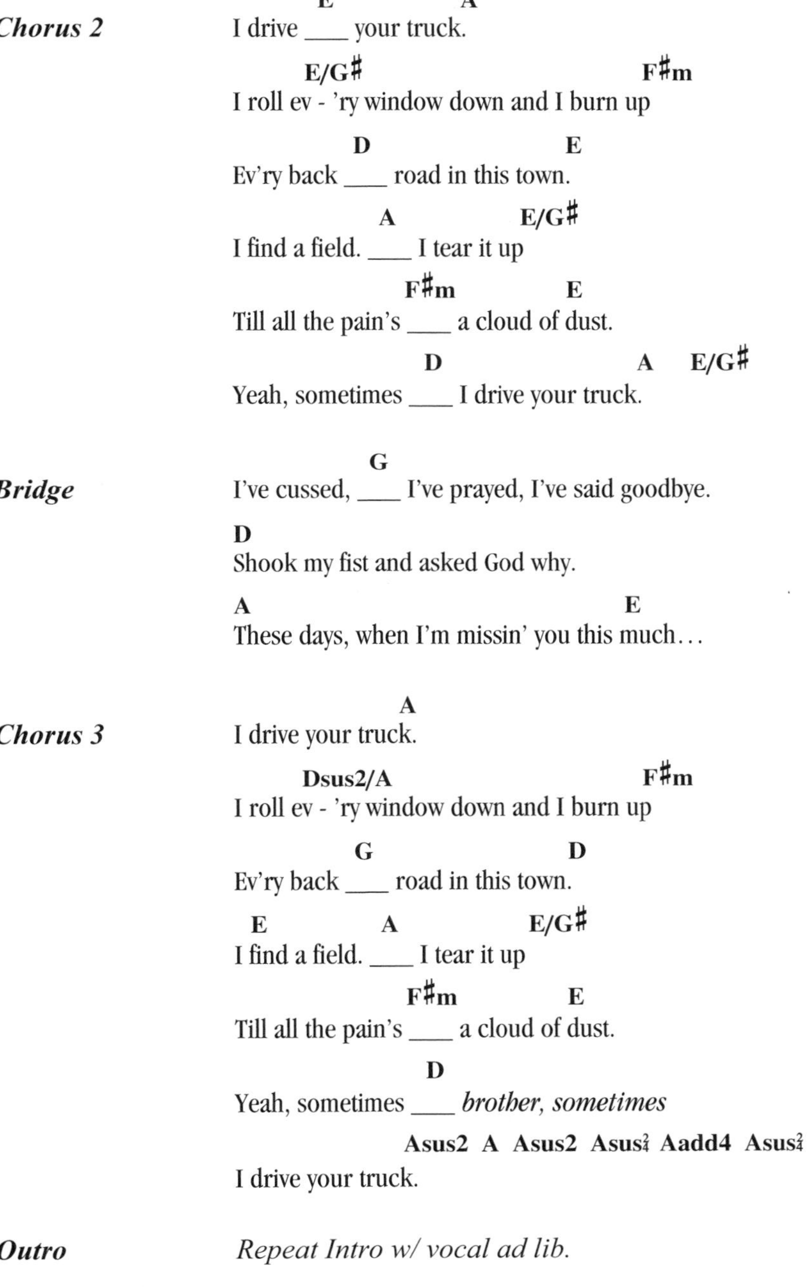

Chorus 2

E A
I drive ___ your truck.

E/G♯ F♯m
I roll ev - 'ry window down and I burn up

D E
Ev'ry back ___ road in this town.

A E/G♯
I find a field. ___ I tear it up

F♯m E
Till all the pain's ___ a cloud of dust.

D A E/G♯
Yeah, sometimes ___ I drive your truck.

Bridge

G
I've cussed, ___ I've prayed, I've said goodbye.

D
Shook my fist and asked God why.

A E
These days, when I'm missin' you this much…

Chorus 3

A
I drive your truck.

Dsus2/A F♯m
I roll ev - 'ry window down and I burn up

G D
Ev'ry back ___ road in this town.

E A E/G♯
I find a field. ___ I tear it up

F♯m E
Till all the pain's ___ a cloud of dust.

D
Yeah, sometimes ___ *brother, sometimes*

Asus2 A Asus2 Asus$^{2}_{4}$ Aadd4 Asus$^{2}_{4}$
I drive your truck.

Outro *Repeat Intro w/ vocal ad lib.*

I Knew You Were Trouble

Words and Music by Taylor Swift,
Shellback and Max Martin

(Capo 6th fret)

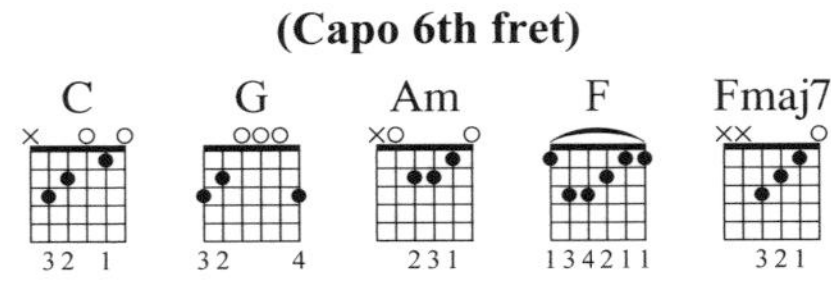

Intro | C | |

Verse 1

```
C
Once upon a time, a few mistakes ago,
G
I was in your sights, you got me alone.
    Am                             F
You found me, you found me, you found me, e, e, e, e.
 C
I guess you didn't care, and I guess I liked that.
    G
And when I fell hard you took a step back,
       Am                          F
With - out me, without me, with - out me, e, e, e, e.
```

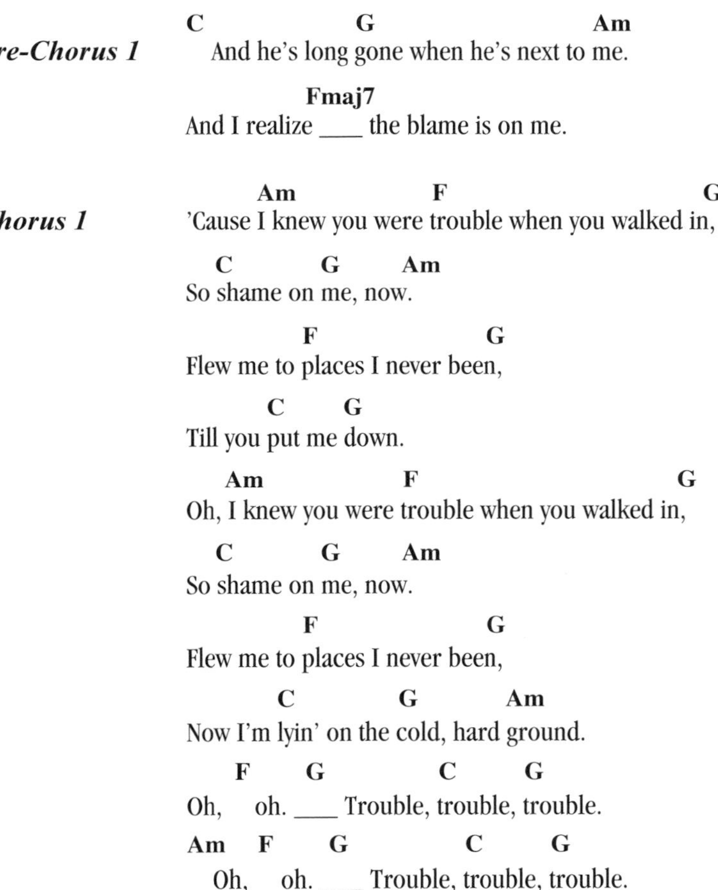

Pre-Chorus 1

```
C                G                          Am
   And he's long gone when he's next to me.
             Fmaj7
And I realize ___ the blame is on me.
```

Chorus 1

```
        Am                F                              G
'Cause I knew you were trouble when you walked in,
   C          G        Am
So shame on me, now.
             F                    G
Flew me to places I never been,
         C       G
Till you put me down.
    Am                 F                             G
Oh, I knew you were trouble when you walked in,
   C          G        Am
So shame on me, now.
             F                    G
Flew me to places I never been,
          C            G            Am
Now I'm lyin' on the cold, hard ground.
     F       G               C         G
Oh,     oh. ___ Trouble, trouble, trouble.
Am     F       G               C         G
   Oh,     oh. ___ Trouble, trouble, trouble.
```

Verse 2

```
C
No apologies, he'll never see you cry.

        G
Pre - tends he doesn't know that he's the reason why

          Am                                   F
You're drowning, you're drowning, you're drown-i-i-i-ing.

        C
And I heard you moved on from whispers on the street.

   G
A new notch in your belt is all I'll ever be.

      Am                   F
And now I see, now I see, now I see, e, e, e, e.
```

Pre-Chorus 2

```
C               G               Am
   He was long gone when he met me.

                F
And I realize ___ the joke is on me. Hey!
```

Chorus 2

Repeat Chorus 1

Bridge

```
           F                  Am
And the saddest fear comes creepin' in

            F
That you never loved me, or her,

    G
Or anyone, or anything. Ah, yeah.
```

```
                Am              F                          G
Chorus 3        I knew you were trouble when you walked in,

                   C          G        Am
                So shame on me, now.

                           F                  G
                Flew me to places I never been,

                          C      G
                Till you put me down.

                    Am              F                          G
                Oh, I knew you were trouble when you walked in,

                   C          G        Am
                So shame on me, now.

                           F                  G
                Flew me to places I never been,

                          C             G            Am
                Now I'm lyin' on the cold, hard ground.

                     F      G             C        G
                Oh,    oh. ___ Trouble, trouble, trouble.

                Am   F      G             C        G
                   Oh,    oh. ___ Trouble, trouble, trouble.

                Am              F                          G
                I knew you were trouble when you walked in,

                          C      G
                Trouble, trouble, trouble.

                Am              F                          G
                I knew you were trouble when you walked in,

                          C      N.C.
                Trouble, trouble, trouble.
```

I Won't Let Go

Words and Music by
Jason Sellers and Steve Robson

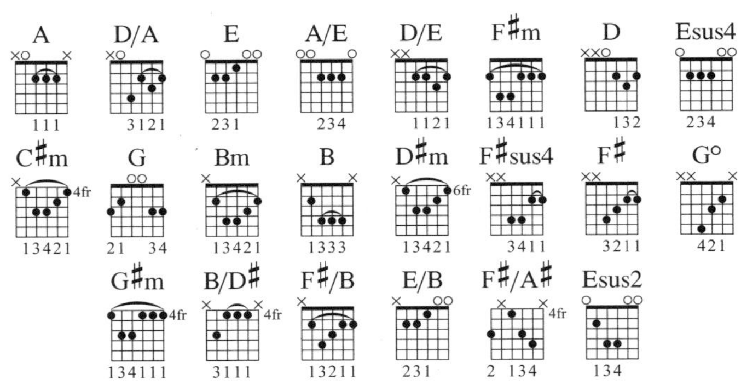

Intro | **A D/A** |

Verse 1

A D/A A D/A A
It's like a storm ___ that cuts a path.

E A/E E
It breaks ___ your will, it feels like that.

D/E F♯m
You think you're lost

D A/E
But you're not lost, on your own.

Esus4 E
You're not alone.

Chorus 1

A C♯m
I will stand by you. I will help you through

D Esus4 E
When you've done all you can do and you can't cope.

F♯m C♯m
I will dry your eyes. I will fight your fight.

D Esus4 E A D/A
I will hold you tight and I won't let go.

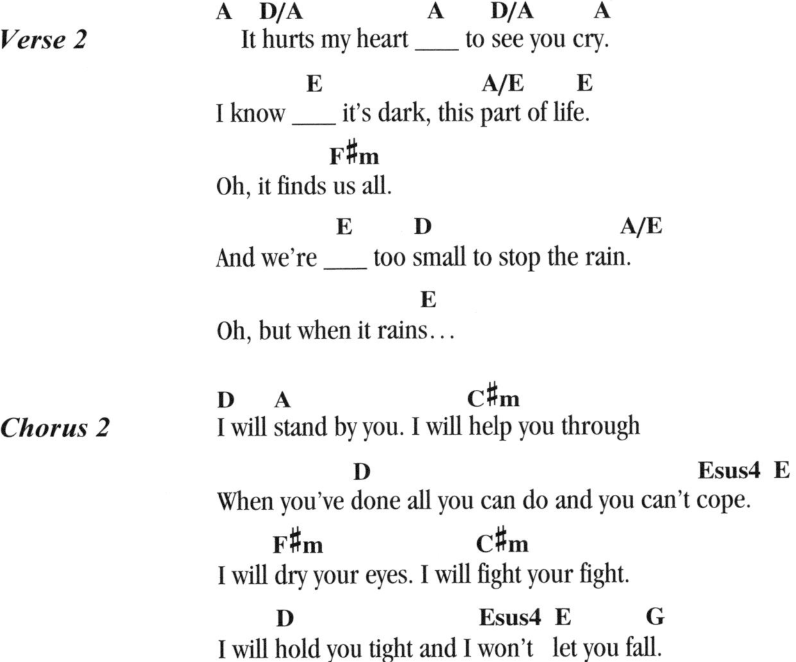

```
            A   D/A              A     D/A      A
Verse 2        It hurts my heart ___ to see you cry.

                    E                  A/E     E
            I know ___ it's dark, this part of life.

                       F#m
            Oh, it finds us all.

                        E       D                    A/E
            And we're ___ too small to stop the rain.

                                E
            Oh, but when it rains…

            D   A                   C#m
Chorus 2    I will stand by you. I will help you through

                            D                              Esus4  E
            When you've done all you can do and you can't cope.

                  F#m                  C#m
            I will dry your eyes. I will fight your fight.

                  D                    Esus4  E      G
            I will hold you tight and I won't  let you fall.
```

Bridge

G **Bm**
Don't be afraid to fall.

A
I'm right here to catch ___ you.

G
I won't let you down.

Bm
It won't get you down.

Esus4
You're gonna make ___ it.

E
Yeah, I know you can make ___ it.

Chorus 3

B **D#m**
'Cause I will stand by you. I will help you through

E **F#sus4 F#**
When you've done all you can do and you can't cope.

G° G#m **D#m**
And I will dry your eyes. I will fight your fight.

E **F#sus4 G° G#m F# E**
I will hold you tight and I won't let go.

B/D# **C#m**
Oh, I'm gonna hold you,

F#sus4 F# B F#/B E/B B
And I won't let go.

F#/A# G#m
Won't let you go.

F# **Esus2**
No, I won't.

If I Die Young

Words and Music by
Kimberly Perry

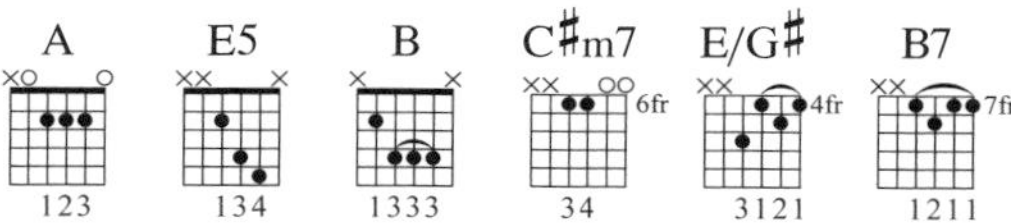

Chorus 1

A E5
If I die young, bury me in satin,
B C♯m7
Lay me down on a bed of ros - es.
A E5
Sink me in the river at dawn,
B C♯m7
Send me a - way with the words of a love song.
A E5 B E/G♯ B7
Uh, oh, ___ uh, oh.

Verse 1

A E5
Lord, make me a rainbow, I'll shine down on my mother.
B C♯m7
She'll know I'm safe with you when she stands under my colors.
A E5
Oh, and life ain't always what you think it oughta be.
B C♯m7
No, ain't even gray but she buries her baby.
A E5 B C♯m7
The sharp knife of a short life,
A E5 B E/G♯ B7
Oh well, I've had just enough time.

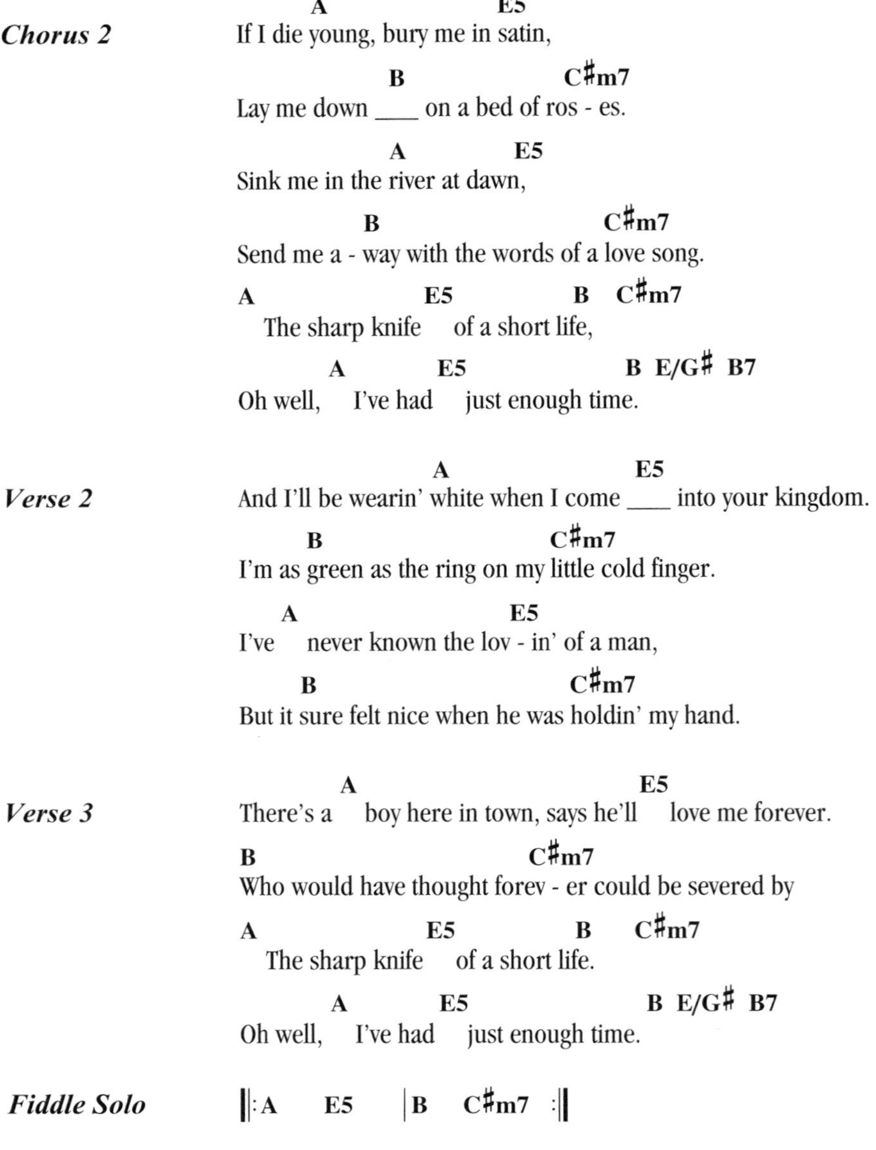

Chorus 2

A E5
If I die young, bury me in satin,

B C#m7
Lay me down ___ on a bed of ros - es.

A E5
Sink me in the river at dawn,

B C#m7
Send me a - way with the words of a love song.

A E5 B C#m7
The sharp knife of a short life,

A E5 B E/G# B7
Oh well, I've had just enough time.

Verse 2

A E5
And I'll be wearin' white when I come ___ into your kingdom.

B C#m7
I'm as green as the ring on my little cold finger.

A E5
I've never known the lov - in' of a man,

B C#m7
But it sure felt nice when he was holdin' my hand.

Verse 3

A E5
There's a boy here in town, says he'll love me forever.

B C#m7
Who would have thought forev - er could be severed by

A E5 B C#m7
The sharp knife of a short life.

A E5 B E/G# B7
Oh well, I've had just enough time.

Fiddle Solo

||: A E5 | B C#m7 :||

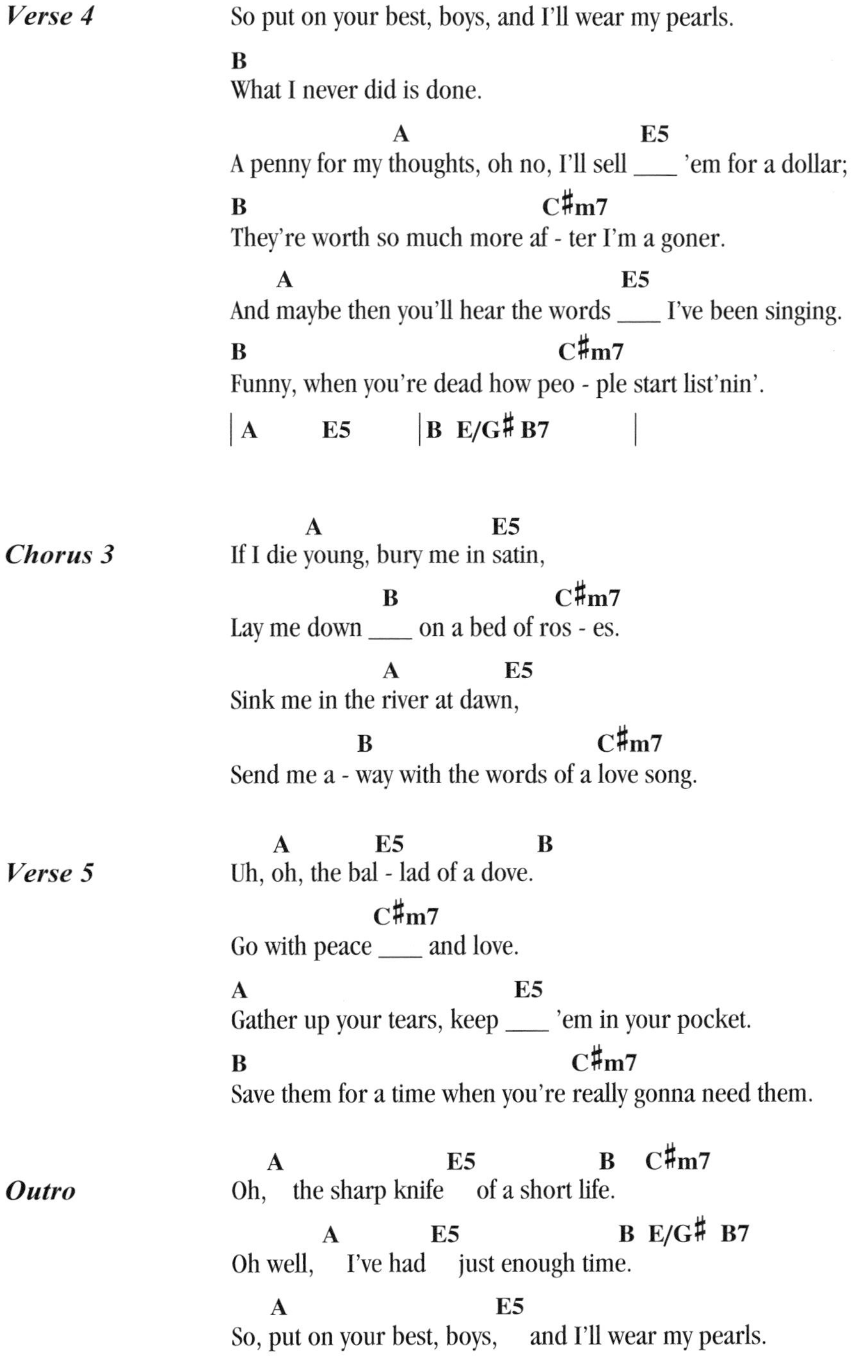

```
                A                                E5
Verse 4    So put on your best, boys, and I'll wear my pearls.

           B
           What I never did is done.

                         A                             E5
           A penny for my thoughts, oh no, I'll sell ___ 'em for a dollar;

           B                            C#m7
           They're worth so much more af - ter I'm a goner.

             A                                     E5
           And maybe then you'll hear the words ___ I've been singing.

           B                             C#m7
           Funny, when you're dead how peo - ple start list'nin'.

           | A        E5        | B  E/G# B7          |


                  A                      E5
Chorus 3   If I die young, bury me in satin,

                       B                    C#m7
           Lay me down ___ on a bed of ros - es.

                       A            E5
           Sink me in the river at dawn,

                     B                        C#m7
           Send me a - way with the words of a love song.


             A          E5                B
Verse 5    Uh, oh, the bal - lad of a dove.

                      C#m7
           Go with peace ___ and love.

           A                          E5
           Gather up your tears, keep ___ 'em in your pocket.

           B                                 C#m7
           Save them for a time when you're really gonna need them.


             A                  E5                  B    C#m7
Outro      Oh,    the sharp knife    of a short life.

                  A           E5                   B  E/G#  B7
           Oh well,     I've had     just enough time.

             A                     E5
           So, put on your best, boys,     and I'll wear my pearls.
```

It's a Great Day to Be Alive

Words and Music by
Darrell Scott

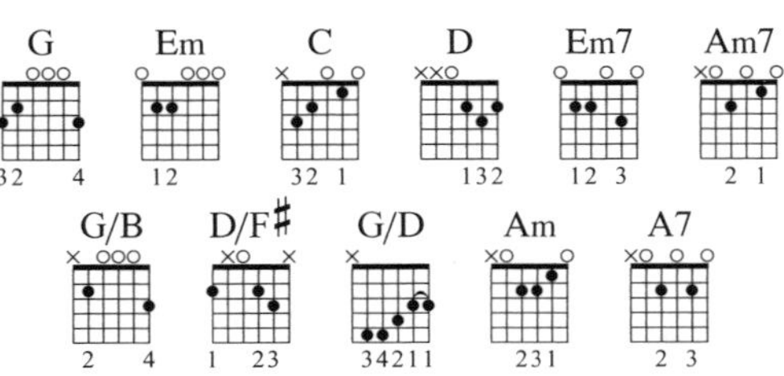

Verse 1

G Em C G
I got a rice cookin' in the microwave.
D Em C
Got a three day beard, I don't plan to shave.
G D Em7 C
And it's a goofy thing, but I just gotta say,
D C G
Hey, I'm a doin' al - right.

Verse 2

G Em C G
Yeah, I think I'll make me some home - made soup.
D Em C
Feelin' pretty good and that's the truth.
G D Em C
It's neither drink nor drug ___ in - duced,
D C G
No, ___ I'm just doin' al - right.

Chorus 1

```
              D           Em7
And it's a great day to be alive.

               Am7     G/B
I know the sun's still shinin'

        C       D
When I close my eyes.

               N.C.  D                 Em7
There's some       hard times in the neighborhood,

          Am7          G/B
But why ___ can't ev'ry day be

C               G  G/B  C  G  D   C
Just this good?
```

Verse 3

```
            G            G/B          C           G
It's been fifteen years ___ since I ___ left home

      D                        Em      C
And said good luck to ev'ry seed I'd sown.

G              D/F#            Em        C
   Give it my best and then I left it alone.

D                 C        G
   I hope they're doin' al - right.
```

Verse 4

```
          G           G/B          C          G
Now, I look in the mirror and what do I see?

    D                         Em      C
A lone wolf there starin' back at me.

G                D/F#            Em             C
   Long in the tooth, but harm - less as can be.

        D                C          G
Lord, ___ I guess he's doin' al - right.
```

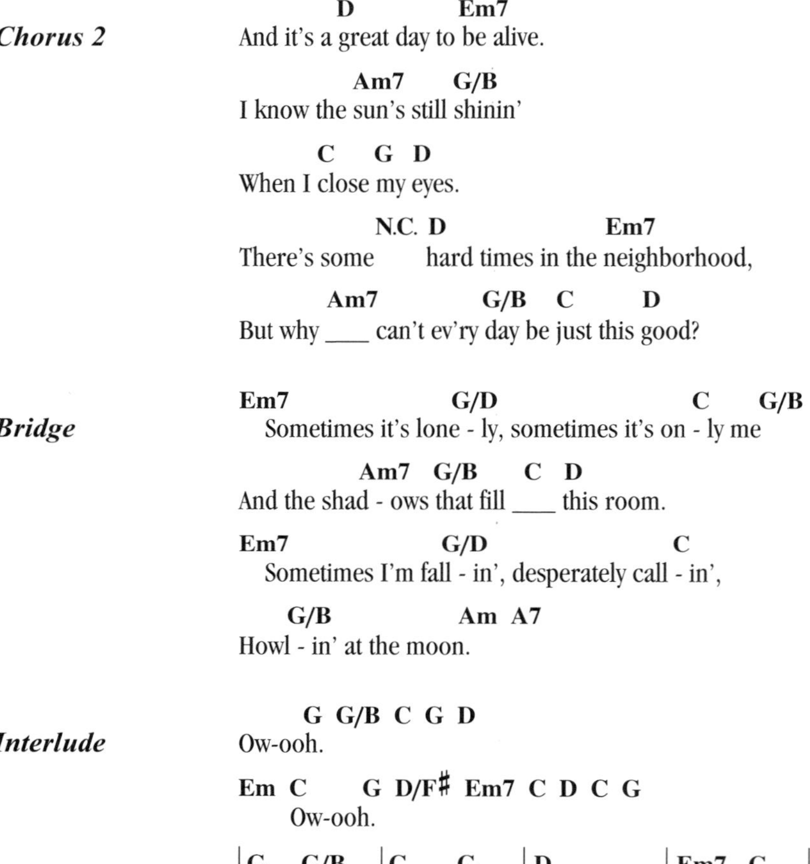

```
                   D             Em7
Chorus 2        And it's a great day to be alive.

                     Am7      G/B
                I know the sun's still shinin'

                     C     G  D
                When I close my eyes.

                             N.C.  D                    Em7
                There's some        hard times in the neighborhood,

                          Am7              G/B    C        D
                But why ___ can't ev'ry day be just this good?

                Em7                    G/D                     C      G/B
Bridge             Sometimes it's lone - ly, sometimes it's on - ly me

                              Am7   G/B      C   D
                And the shad - ows that fill ___ this room.

                Em7                    G/D                     C
                   Sometimes I'm fall - in', desperately call - in',

                     G/B               Am  A7
                Howl - in' at the moon.

                        G  G/B  C  G  D
Interlude       Ow-ooh.

                Em  C      G  D/F#  Em7  C  D  C  G
                      Ow-ooh.

                | G    G/B   | C      G    | D          | Em7   C   |
                | G    D/F#  | Em7    C    | D     C    | G         |
```

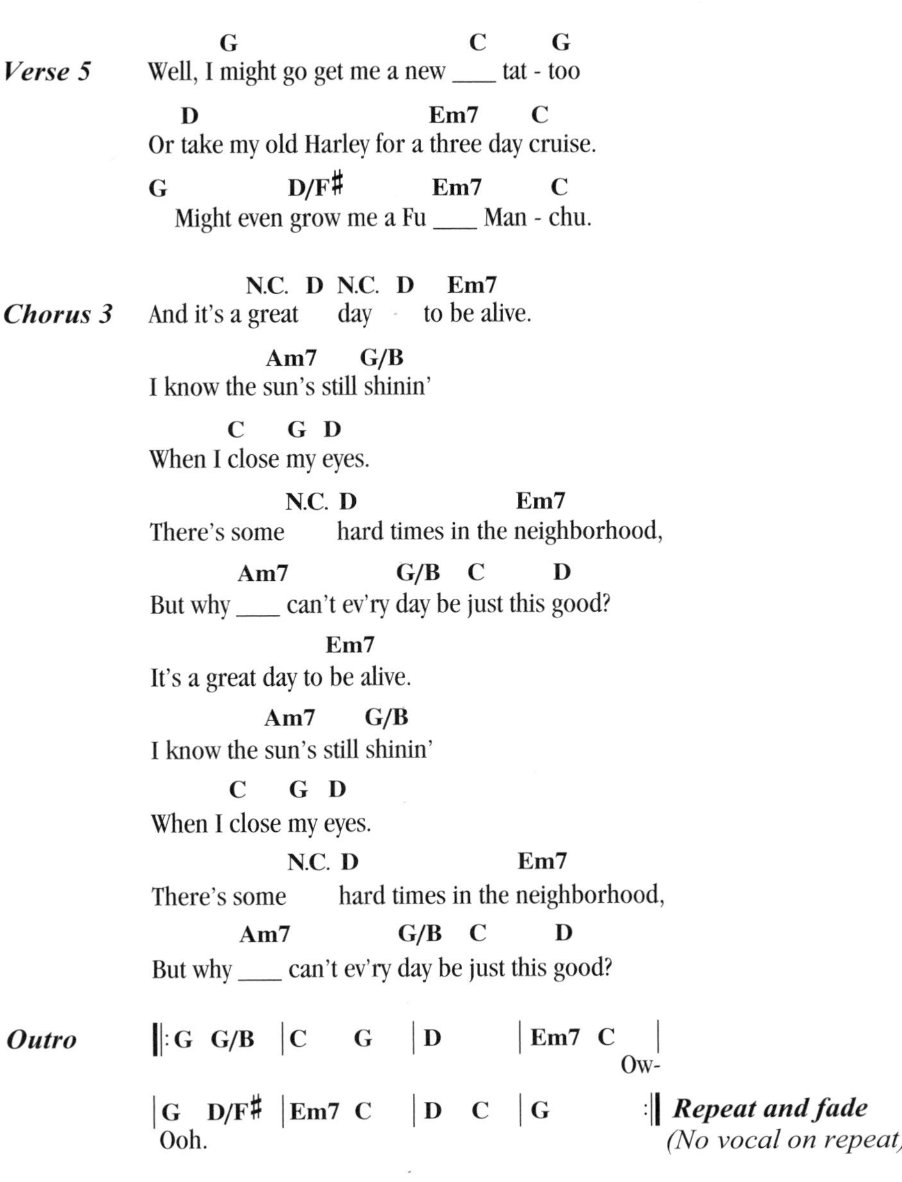

Verse 5

G C G
Well, I might go get me a new ___ tat - too
D Em7 C
Or take my old Harley for a three day cruise.
G D/F♯ Em7 C
Might even grow me a Fu ___ Man - chu.

Chorus 3

N.C. D N.C. D Em7
And it's a great day to be alive.
Am7 G/B
I know the sun's still shinin'
C G D
When I close my eyes.
N.C. D Em7
There's some hard times in the neighborhood,
Am7 G/B C D
But why ___ can't ev'ry day be just this good?
Em7
It's a great day to be alive.
Am7 G/B
I know the sun's still shinin'
C G D
When I close my eyes.
N.C. D Em7
There's some hard times in the neighborhood,
Am7 G/B C D
But why ___ can't ev'ry day be just this good?

Outro

‖: **G G/B** | **C G** | **D** | **Em7 C** |
Ow-
| **G D/F♯** | **Em7 C** | **D C** | **G** :‖ ***Repeat and fade***
Ooh. *(No vocal on repeat)*

Just a Kiss

Words and Music by Hillary Scott,
Dallas Davidson, Charles Kelley
and Dave Haywood

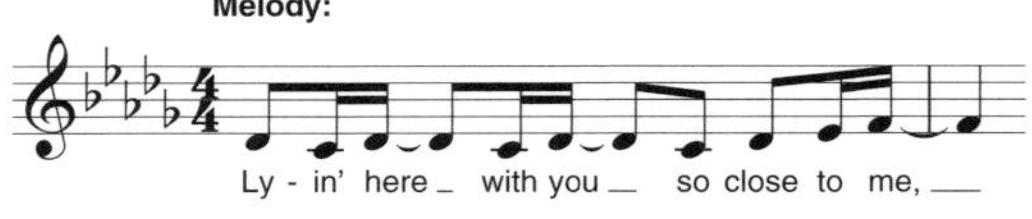

(Capo 1st fret)

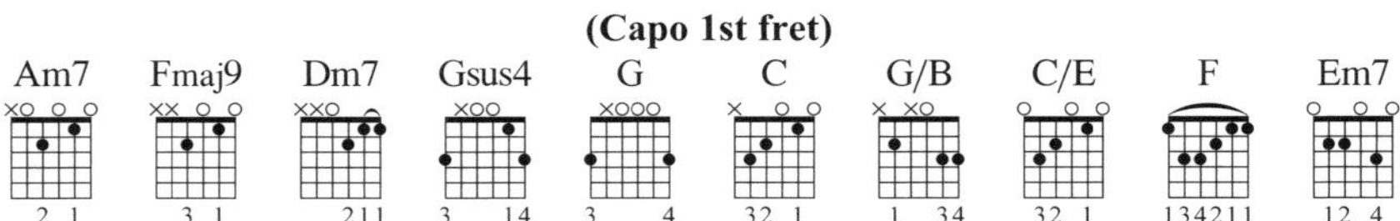


```
Intro           | Am7      | Fmaj9    | Am7      | Fmaj9    |

                  Am7                                 Fmaj9
Verse 1           Lyin' here with you so close to me,

                                             Am7
                  It's hard to fight these feel   -   ings

                                                    Fmaj9
                  When it feels so hard to breathe.

                                               Dm7
                  I'm caught up in this mo   -   ment,

                                            Gsus4        G
                  I'm caught up in your smile.


                     Am7                            Fmaj9
Verse 2           I've never opened up to anyone.

                  So hard to hold back

                  Am7                                 Fmaj9
                  When I'm holding you in my arms.

                                            Dm7
                  We don't need to rush        this;

                                            Gsus4        G
                  Let's just take it slow.
```

Chorus 1

```
Am7                 Fmaj9
  Just a kiss on your lips in the moonlight,

C                   G/B
  Just a touch of the fire burning so bright.

Am7                 Fmaj9
  No, I don't want to mess this thing up.

Gsus4               G
  No, I don't want to push too far.

Am7               Fmaj9
  Just a shot in the dark that you just might

C                         G/B                 Dm7
  Be the one I've been waiting for my whole      life.

           C/E      F
So baby, I'm   alright

          G           Am7          Fmaj9
With just a kiss good - night.
```

Verse 3

```
  Am7                                   Fmaj9
I know that if we give this a little time,

                         Am7
It'll only bring us clos  -  er

                              Fmaj9
To the love we wanna find.

                         Dm7
It's never felt so real,

                              Gsus4       G
No, it's never felt so right.
```

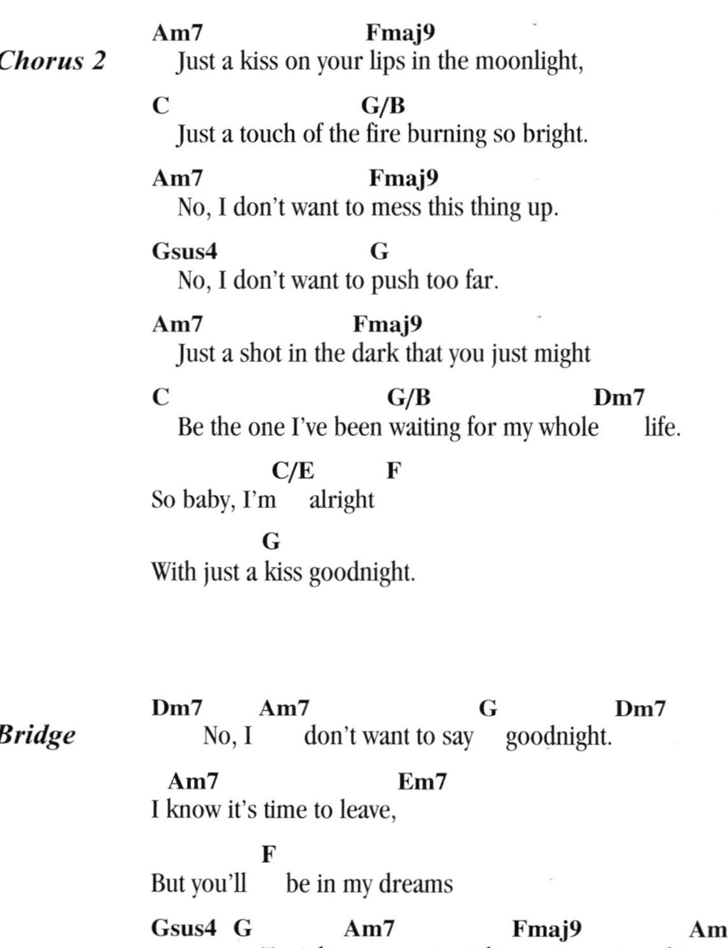

Chorus 2

Am7 Fmaj9
Just a kiss on your lips in the moonlight,

C G/B
Just a touch of the fire burning so bright.

Am7 Fmaj9
No, I don't want to mess this thing up.

Gsus4 G
No, I don't want to push too far.

Am7 Fmaj9
Just a shot in the dark that you just might

C G/B Dm7
Be the one I've been waiting for my whole life.

C/E F
So baby, I'm alright

G
With just a kiss goodnight.

Bridge

Dm7 Am7 G Dm7
No, I don't want to say goodnight.

Am7 Em7
I know it's time to leave,

F
But you'll be in my dreams

Gsus4 G Am7 Fmaj9 Am7
Tonight, tonight, tonight.

```
             Am7                   Fmaj9
Chorus 3       Just a kiss on your lips in the moonlight,

             C                     G/B
               Just a touch of the fire burning so bright.

             Am7                   Fmaj9
               No, I don't want to mess this thing up.

             Gsus4                 G
               No, I don't want to push too far.

             Am7                 Fmaj9
               Just a shot in the dark that you just might

             C                        G/B                     Dm7
               Be the one I've been waiting for my whole     life.

                            C/E   F         G
             So baby, I'm al    -   right,

                 Dm7          C/E          F
             Oh,        let's do    this right,

                          G            Am7
             With just a kiss good - night,

             Fmaj9                     Am7
                 With a kiss goodnight,

                             F
             Kiss goodnight.
```

Little Bit of Everything

Words and Music by Brad Warren,
Brett Warren and Kevin Rudolph

(Capo 3rd fret)

F Bbsus2 C Gm7 Bb Dm

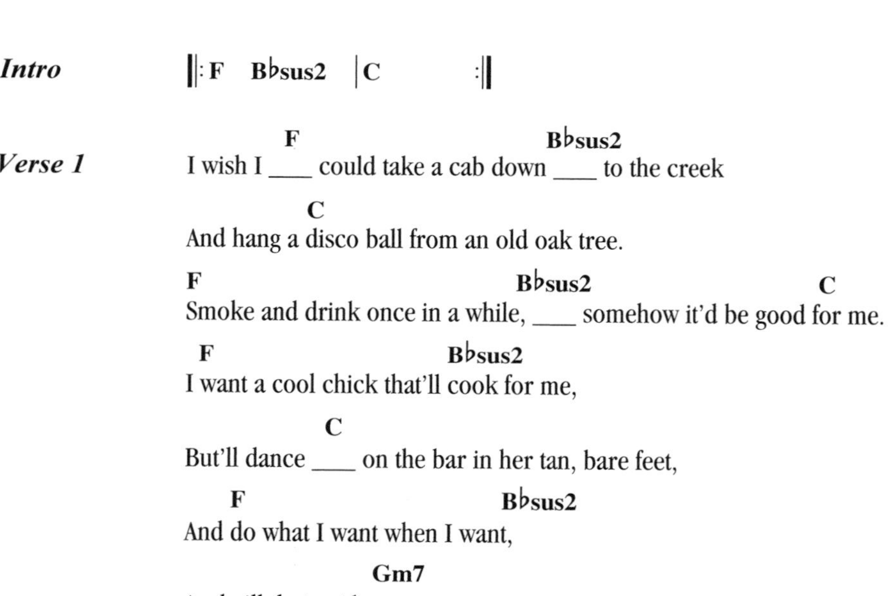

Intro

|: **F** **Bbsus2** | **C** :|

Verse 1

F **Bbsus2**
I wish I ___ could take a cab down ___ to the creek

C
And hang a disco ball from an old oak tree.

F **Bbsus2** **C**
Smoke and drink once in a while, ___ somehow it'd be good for me.

F **Bbsus2**
I want a cool chick that'll cook for me,

C
But'll dance ___ on the bar in her tan, bare feet,

F **Bbsus2**
And do what I want when I want,

Gm7
A, she'll do it with ___ me, mm.

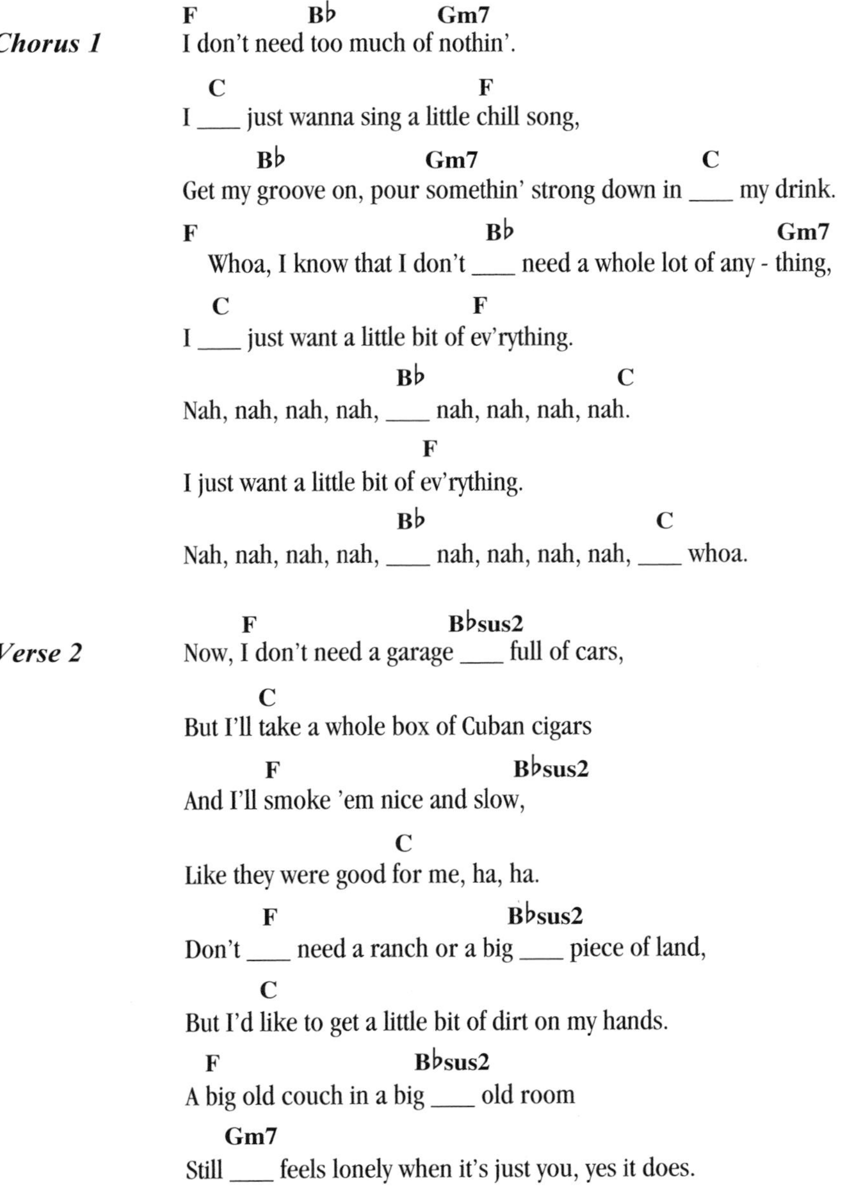

Chorus 1

F **Bb** **Gm7**
I don't need too much of nothin'.

C **F**
I ___ just wanna sing a little chill song,

Bb **Gm7** **C**
Get my groove on, pour somethin' strong down in ___ my drink.

F **Bb** **Gm7**
Whoa, I know that I don't ___ need a whole lot of any - thing,

C **F**
I ___ just want a little bit of ev'rything.

Bb **C**
Nah, nah, nah, nah, ___ nah, nah, nah, nah.

F
I just want a little bit of ev'rything.

Bb **C**
Nah, nah, nah, nah, ___ nah, nah, nah, nah, ___ whoa.

Verse 2

F **Bbsus2**
Now, I don't need a garage ___ full of cars,

C
But I'll take a whole box of Cuban cigars

F **Bbsus2**
And I'll smoke 'em nice and slow,

C
Like they were good for me, ha, ha.

F **Bbsus2**
Don't ___ need a ranch or a big ___ piece of land,

C
But I'd like to get a little bit of dirt on my hands.

F **Bbsus2**
A big old couch in a big ___ old room

Gm7
Still ___ feels lonely when it's just you, yes it does.

```
             F            B♭           Gm7
Chorus 2     I don't need too much of nothin'.

              C                       F
             I ___ just wanna sing a little chill song,

                B♭              Gm7                       C
             Get my groove on, pour somethin' strong down in ___ my drink.

             F                             B♭                      Gm7
               Whoa, I know that I don't ___ need a whole lot of any - thing,

              C                       F
             I ___ just want a little bit of ev'rything.

                                 B♭                  C
             Nah, nah, nah, nah, ___ nah, nah, nah, nah.


                         Dm                   F
Bridge       A little bit of ev'rything under the sun.

                         B♭
             So when I kick back, baskin' in it,

                          C
             I'll be okay ___ with what I've done, still havin' fun.
```

Interlude *Repeat Intro*

```
                 F              B♭            Gm7
Chorus 3         'Cause I don't need too much of nothin'.

                   C
                 I ___ just wanna sing a little chill song,

                                  N.C.                   C
                 Get my groove on, pour somethin' strong down in ___ my drink.
                 F                          B♭                        Gm7
                    Whoa, I know that I don't ___ need a whole lot of any - thing,
                   C                        F
                 I ___ just want a little bit of ev'rything.
                              B♭                C
                 Nah, nah, nah, nah, ___ nah, nah, nah, nah.
                                F
                 I just want a little bit of ev'rything.
                              B♭                C
                 Nah, nah, nah, nah, ___ nah, nah, nah, nah.
                                F           B♭
                 I just want a little bit of ev'rything, yeah.
                 C                   F  B♭  C
                    Whoa, whoa, whoa, yeah.

Outro-Guitar Solo ||: F   B♭sus2  | C        :|| Repeat and fade
```

Making Memories of Us

Words and Music by
Rodney Crowell

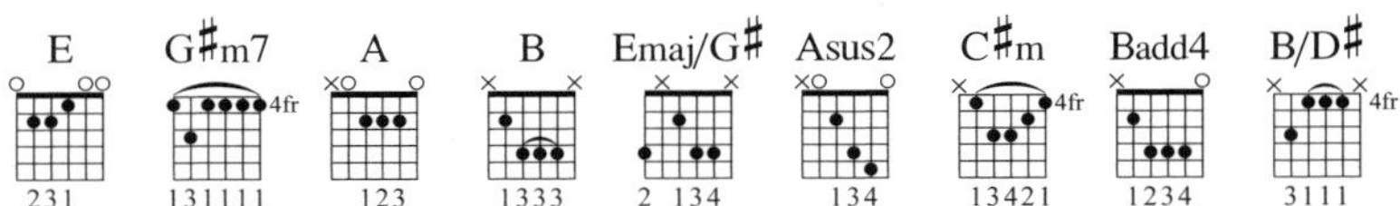

Intro ‖: E | | G#m7 | A :‖

Verse 1

```
E                                B
   I'm gonna be here for you, ba - by.
Emaj7/G#                 Asus2
   I'll be a man of my word.
E                             B
   Speak the language in a voice
                   C#m        B  A
That you have never ___ heard.
E                              Badd4
   I wanna sleep with you for - ever
Emaj7/G#                     A
   And I wanna die in your arms
E                      B
   In a cabin by a mea - dow
                   C#m           B  A
Where the wild bees ___ swarm.
```

Chorus 1

```
A                        E       A              E
   And I'm gonna love ___ you    like nobody loves you.
A                          C#m          B            E
   And I'll earn your trust ___ making mem'ries of ___ us.
```

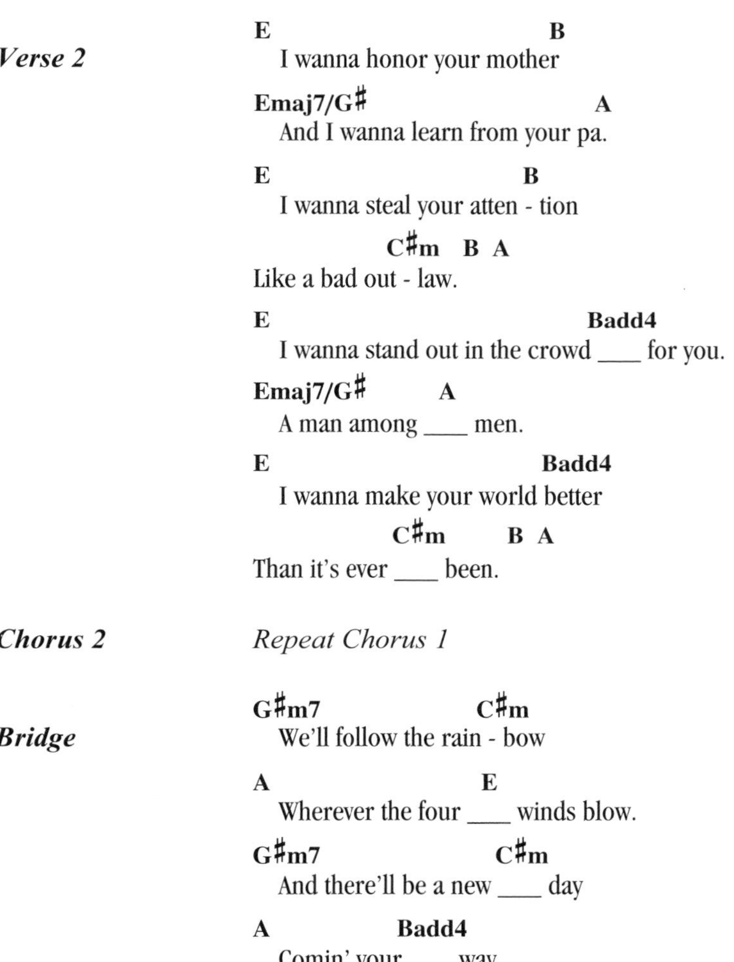

Verse 2

E B
I wanna honor your mother
Emaj7/G# A
And I wanna learn from your pa.
E B
I wanna steal your atten - tion
C#m B A
Like a bad out - law.
E Badd4
I wanna stand out in the crowd ___ for you.
Emaj7/G# A
A man among ___ men.
E Badd4
I wanna make your world better
C#m B A
Than it's ever ___ been.

Chorus 2

Repeat Chorus 1

Bridge

G#m7 C#m
We'll follow the rain - bow
A E
Wherever the four ___ winds blow.
G#m7 C#m
And there'll be a new ___ day
A Badd4
Comin' your ___ way.

```
            E                        B
Verse 3       I'm gonna be here for you from now on.

            Emaj7/G#                 Asus2
              This you know somehow.

            E                              B
              You've been stretched to the lim - its

                         C#m        B  A
            But it's alright ____ now.

            E                                       Badd4
              And I'm gonna make you a promise,

            Emaj7/G#                 A
              If there's life after this

            E                            B
              I'm gonna be there to meet ____ you

                             C#m        B  A
            With a warm, wet ____ kiss.


            A                        E        A            E
Chorus 3      And I'm gonna love ____ you     like nobody loves you.

            A                          C#m         B           E
              And I'll earn your trust ____ making mem'ries of ____ us.

            A                        E        A            E
              And I'm gonna love ____ you     like nobody loves you.

            A                     C#m         B/D#          E       G#m7  A
              And I'll win your trust making mem'ries of ____ us.

            | E         |         | G#m7     | A         | E         ||
```

Remind Me

Words and Music by Kelley Lovelace,
Brad Paisley and Chris DuBois

(Capo 1st fret)

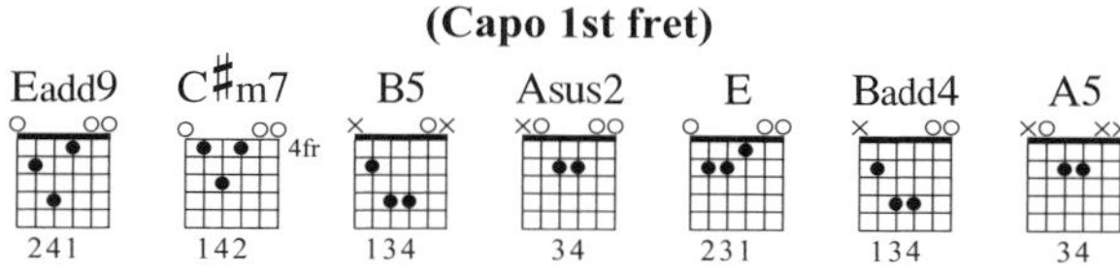

Intro ‖: **Eadd9** | **C#m7** | **B5** | **Asus2** :‖

Verse 1

```
                   Eadd9
Brad Paisley: We didn't care if people stared.
C#m7
We'd make out in a crowd somewhere.
B5
Somebody'd tell us to get a room.
   Asus2
It's hard to believe that was me and you.
     Eadd9
Now, we keep sayin' that we're okay.
   C#m7
But I don't wanna settle for good, not great.
     B5
Now, I miss the way that it felt back then.
        Asus2
I wanna feel that way again.
```

Chorus 1

```
E                                          C#m7
Been so long that you'd forget the way ___ I used to kiss your neck.

                                    Badd4            Asus2
Carrie Underwood: Remind ___ me, remind ___ me.

           E
Brad: So ___ on fire, so in love.

   C#m7
Way ___ back when we couldn't get enough.

                Badd4            Asus2
Carrie: Remind ___ me, remind ___ me.
```

Verse 2

```
              Eadd9
Carrie: Re - member the airport, droppin' me off?

           C#m7
We were kissin' goodbye and we couldn't stop.

        B5
Brad: I felt bad 'cause you missed your flight,

           A5
Both: But that meant we had one more night.
```

Chorus 2

```
            E
Carrie: Do you remember how it used to be?

             C#m7
We turned ___ out the lights and we didn't just sleep.

               Badd4                Asus2
Brad: Remind ___ me, baby, remind ___ me.

              E
Carrie: Oh, so on fire and so in love,

             C#m7
That look ___ in your eyes that I miss so much.

               Badd4                Asus2
Both: Remind ___ me, baby, remind ___ me.
```

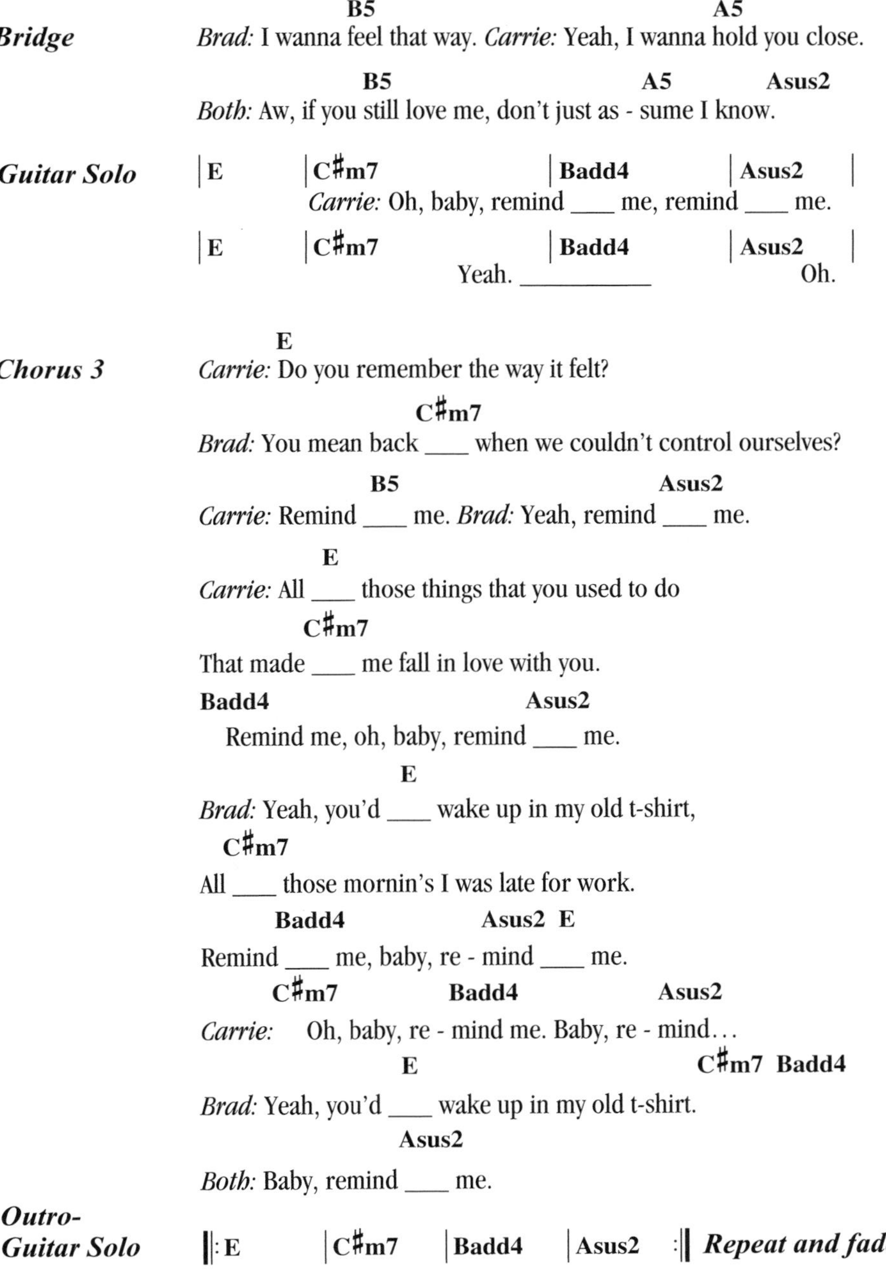

Bridge

B5 A5
Brad: I wanna feel that way. *Carrie:* Yeah, I wanna hold you close.

B5 A5 Asus2
Both: Aw, if you still love me, don't just as - sume I know.

Guitar Solo

| E | C♯m7 | Badd4 | Asus2 |
Carrie: Oh, baby, remind ___ me, remind ___ me.

| E | C♯m7 | Badd4 | Asus2 |
Yeah. __________ Oh.

Chorus 3

E
Carrie: Do you remember the way it felt?

C♯m7
Brad: You mean back ___ when we couldn't control ourselves?

B5 Asus2
Carrie: Remind ___ me. *Brad:* Yeah, remind ___ me.

E
Carrie: All ___ those things that you used to do

C♯m7
That made ___ me fall in love with you.

Badd4 Asus2
Remind me, oh, baby, remind ___ me.

E
Brad: Yeah, you'd ___ wake up in my old t-shirt,

C♯m7
All ___ those mornin's I was late for work.

Badd4 Asus2 E
Remind ___ me, baby, re - mind ___ me.

C♯m7 Badd4 Asus2
Carrie: Oh, baby, re - mind me. Baby, re - mind…

E C♯m7 Badd4
Brad: Yeah, you'd ___ wake up in my old t-shirt.

Asus2
Both: Baby, remind ___ me.

Outro-Guitar Solo

‖: E | C♯m7 | Badd4 | Asus2 :‖ ***Repeat and fade***

Mama's Broken Heart

Words and Music by Shane McAnally,
Brandy Clark and Kacey Musgraves

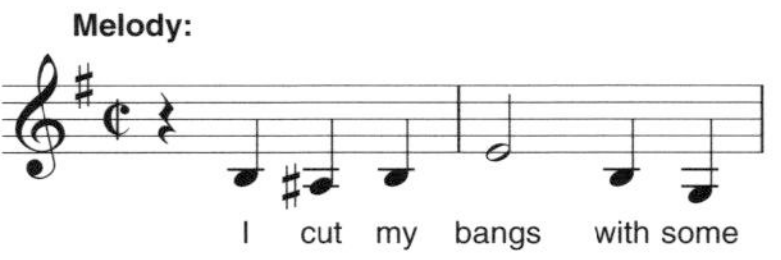

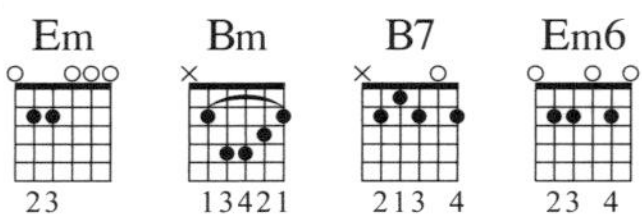

Intro | Em | | | |

Verse 1

Em
I cut my bangs with some rusty kitchen scissors.
Bm
I screamed his name 'til the neighbors called the cops.
Em
I numbed the pain at the expense of my liver.
Bm Em N.C.
Don't know what I did next, all I know, I couldn't stop.

Verse 2

Em
Word got around to the bar flies and the Baptists.
Bm
My mama's phone started ringin' off the hook.
Em
I can hear her now sayin' she ain't gonna have it.
Bm Em
Don't matter how you feel, it only matters how you look.

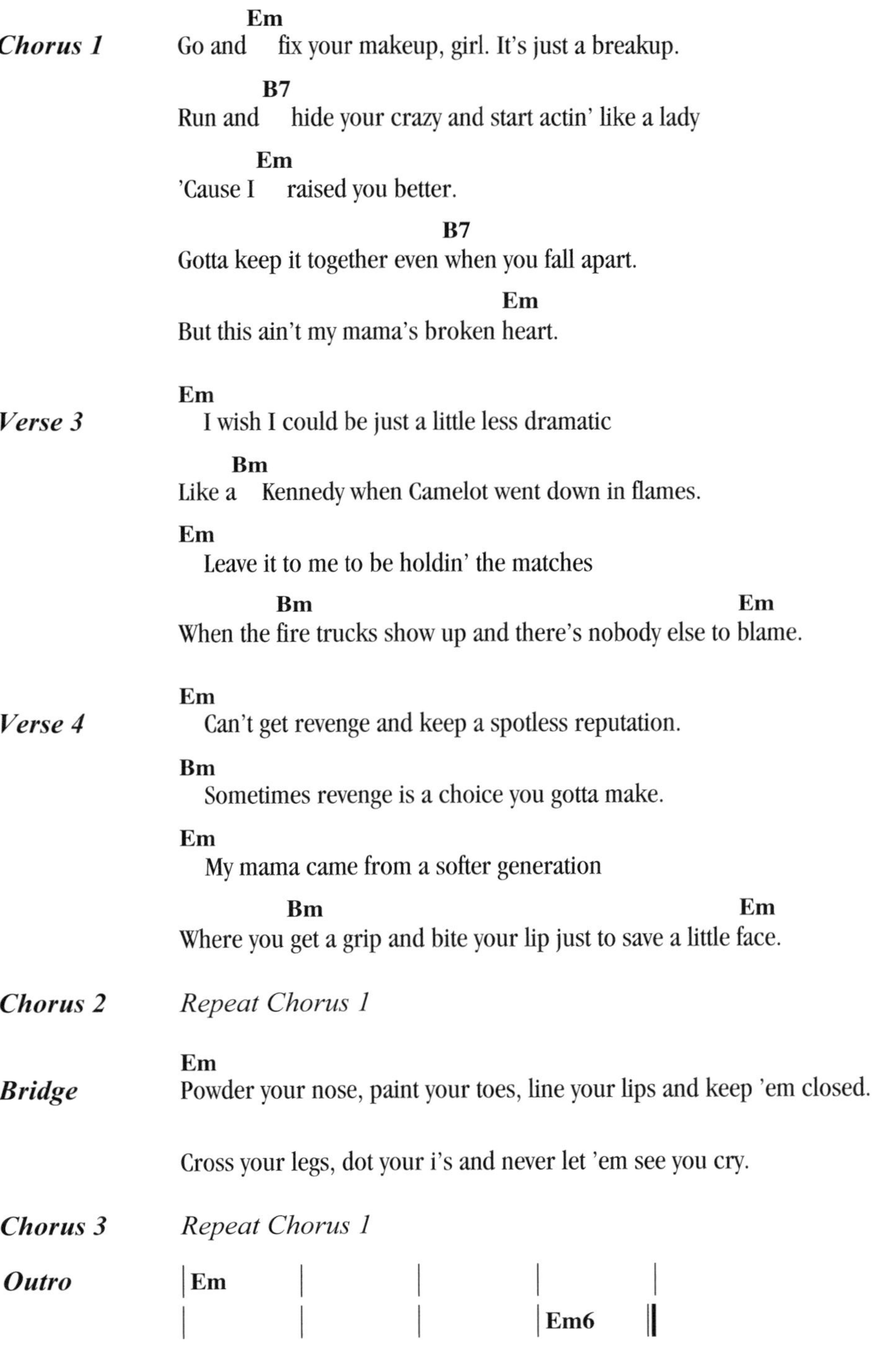
Chorus 1
Em
Go and fix your makeup, girl. It's just a breakup.
B7
Run and hide your crazy and start actin' like a lady
Em
'Cause I raised you better.
B7
Gotta keep it together even when you fall apart.
Em
But this ain't my mama's broken heart.
Verse 3
Em
I wish I could be just a little less dramatic
Bm
Like a Kennedy when Camelot went down in flames.
Em
Leave it to me to be holdin' the matches
Bm
Em
When the fire trucks show up and there's nobody else to blame.
Verse 4
Em
Can't get revenge and keep a spotless reputation.
Bm
Sometimes revenge is a choice you gotta make.
Em
My mama came from a softer generation
Bm
Em
Where you get a grip and bite your lip just to save a little face.
Chorus 2
Repeat Chorus 1
Bridge
Em
Powder your nose, paint your toes, line your lips and keep 'em closed.
Cross your legs, dot your i's and never let 'em see you cry.
Chorus 3
Repeat Chorus 1
Outro
Em
Em6

Merry Go Round

Words and Music by Kacey Musgraves,
Shane McAnally and Josh Osborne

Tune down 1/2 step:
(low to high) E♭-A♭-D♭-G♭-B♭-E♭

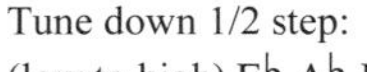

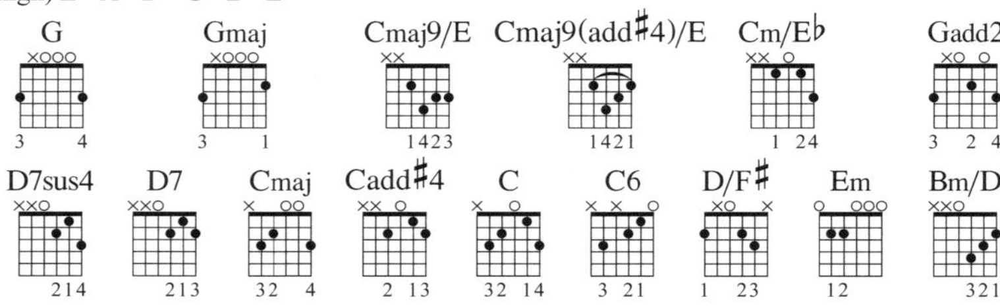

Intro ‖: G Gmaj7 | | G Gmaj7 | :‖

Verse 1

G **Gmaj7** **G**
If you ain't got two kids by twenty-one,

Gmaj7 **Cmaj9/E**
You're prob'bly gonna die alone.

Cmaj9(add♯4)/E **Cmaj9/E** **Cmaj9(add♯4)/E**
'Least that's what ___ tradition told ___ you.

G **Gmaj7** **G**
And it don't matter if you don't believe.

Gmaj7 **Cmaj9/E**
Come Sunday mornin' you best be ___ there

Cmaj9(add♯4)/E **Cmaj9/E** **Cmaj9(add♯4)/E**
In the front row like you're s'posed ___ to.

Cm/E♭ **G Gadd2 G**
Same hurt in ev'ry heart,

Cm/E♭ **D7sus4 D7**
Same trailer, diff'rent park.

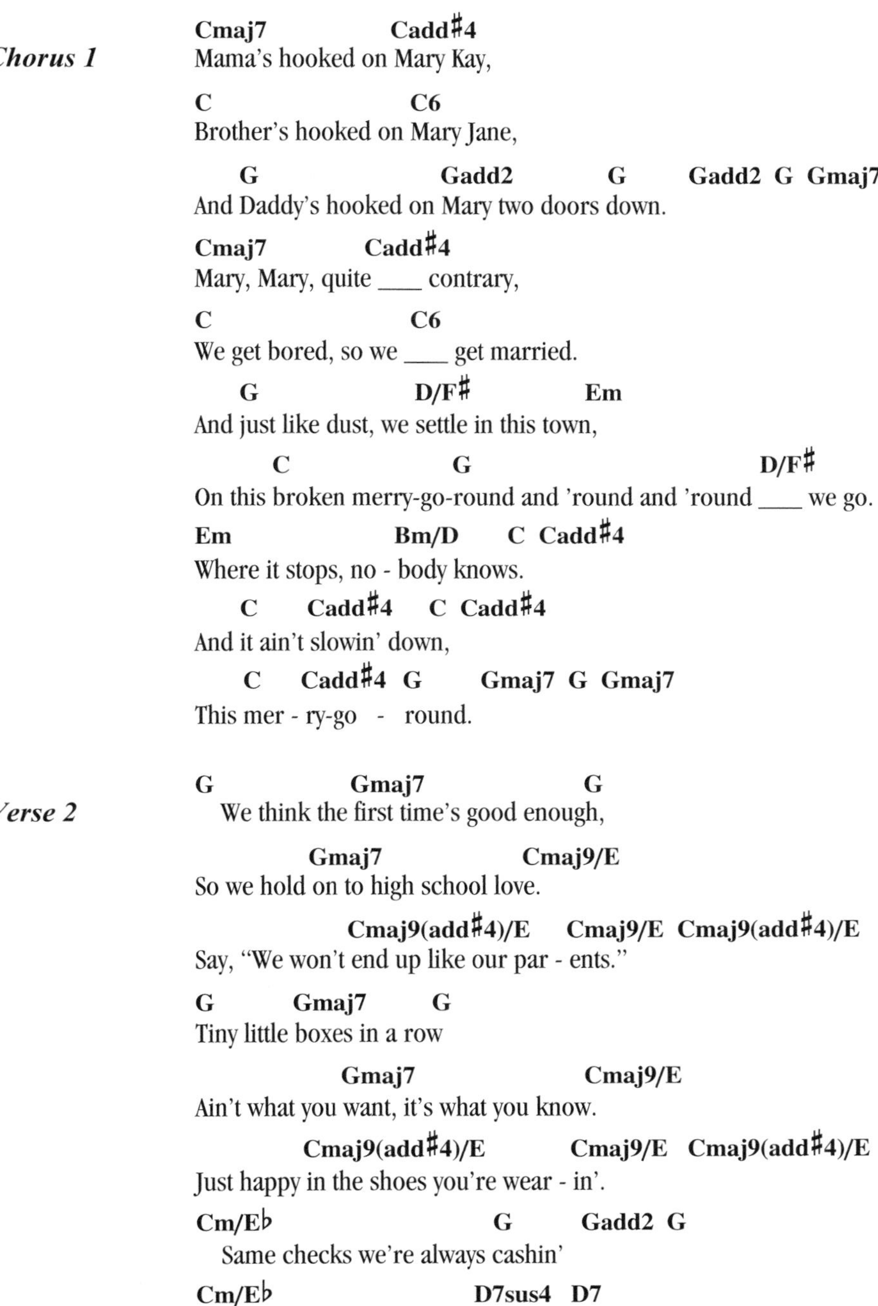

Chorus 1

```
Cmaj7              Cadd♯4
Mama's hooked on Mary Kay,

C                      C6
Brother's hooked on Mary Jane,

    G                    Gadd2          G        Gadd2  G  Gmaj7
And Daddy's hooked on Mary two doors down.

Cmaj7              Cadd♯4
Mary, Mary, quite ___ contrary,

C                      C6
We get bored, so we ___ get married.

    G                D/F♯              Em
And just like dust, we settle in this town,

       C                  G                              D/F♯
On this broken merry-go-round and 'round and 'round ___ we go.

Em                     Bm/D     C  Cadd♯4
Where it stops, no - body knows.

    C      Cadd♯4    C  Cadd♯4
And it ain't slowin' down,

     C    Cadd♯4  G       Gmaj7  G  Gmaj7
This mer - ry-go  -  round.
```

Verse 2

```
G               Gmaj7                 G
   We think the first time's good enough,

            Gmaj7                 Cmaj9/E
So we hold on to high school love.

                 Cmaj9(add♯4)/E    Cmaj9/E  Cmaj9(add♯4)/E
Say, "We won't end up like our par - ents."

G          Gmaj7       G
Tiny little boxes in a row

                 Gmaj7                    Cmaj9/E
Ain't what you want, it's what you know.

            Cmaj9(add♯4)/E            Cmaj9/E  Cmaj9(add♯4)/E
Just happy in the shoes you're wear - in'.

Cm/E♭                          G        Gadd2  G
   Same checks we're always cashin'

Cm/E♭                        D7sus4  D7
   To buy a little more dis - traction.
```

```
             Cmaj7                  Cadd♯4
Chorus 2     'Cause Mama's hooked on Mary Kay,

             C                      C6
             Brother's hooked on Mary Jane,

                 G                    Gadd2          G        Gadd2  G  Gmaj7
             And Daddy's hooked on Mary two doors down.

             Cmaj7            Cadd♯4
             Mary, Mary, quite ___ contrary,

             C                      C6
             We get bored, so we ___ get married.

                 G                 D/F♯             Em
             And just like dust, we settle in this town,

                    C                 G                              D/F♯
             On this broken merry-go-round and 'round and 'round ___ we go.

             Em                  Bm/D       C  Cadd♯4
             Where it stops, no - body knows.

                 C      Cadd♯4    C  Cadd♯4
             And it ain't slowin' down,

                 C      Cadd♯4  G      Gmaj7
             This mer - ry-go  -  round.

             | G   Gmaj7  |        | Cmaj9/E  Cmaj9(add♯4)/E |
             |        | Cmaj9/E  Cmaj9(add♯4)/E |        |
```

Chorus 3

```
Cmaj7           Cadd♯4
Mary, Mary, quite ___ contrary,

C                    C6
We're so bored, until ___ we're buried.

   G               D/F♯          Em
And just like dust, we settle in this town,

      C              G       Gmaj7  G  Gmaj7
On this broken merry-go-round.

           Cmaj9/E  Cmaj9(add♯4)/E   Cmaj9/E  Cmaj9(add♯4)/E
Merry-go-round.
```

Outro

```
G               Gmaj7
Jack and Jill went ___ up the hill.

G                 Gmaj7
Jack burned out on ___ booze and pills.

   Cmaj9/E  Cmaj9(add♯4)/E
And Mary had  a little lamb,

Cmaj9/E    Cmaj9(add♯4)/E    G
Mary just don't ___ give a damn no more.
```

Need You Now

Words and Music by Hillary Scott,
Charles Kelley, Dave Haywood and
Josh Kear

Melody:
Pic-ture per-fect mem - 'ries
scat-tered all a-round

F (321) Am (231) Fmaj7 (T3421) Fmaj7sus2 (T34 1) Asus2 (23) Asus4 (234)

C/G (342 1) Em (12) G/B (2 4) Gsus4 (3 14) G (3 4) Em* (2)

Intro

F		Am	
Fmaj7		Am	

Verse 1

Fmaj7 Am
Female: Picture perfect mem'ries scattered all around the floor.

Fmaj7 Am
Reachin' for the phone 'cause I can't fight it anymore.

Pre-Chorus 1

Fmaj7sus2 Am Asus2
Male & Female: And I won - der if I ever cross your mind.

Asus4 Am Fmaj7sus2
For me it hap - pens all the time.

Chorus 1

C/G Em
Both: It's a quarter after one, I'm all alone and I need ___ you now.

C/G Em
Said ___ I wouldn't call but I lost all control and I need ___ you now.

Fmaj7sus2
And I don't ___ know how I can do without.

I just need you now.

Interlude 1

Fmaj7		Am	

```
                         Fmaj7                                      Am
Verse 2          Male: An - other shot of whiskey, can't stop lookin' at the door,
                     Fmaj7                                      Am
                 Wish - ing you'd come sweeping in the way you did before.

                                          Fmaj7                    Am
Pre-Chorus 1     Male & Female: And I won - der if I ever cross your mind.
                                     Fmaj7
                 Male: For me it hap - pens all the time.

                          C/G
Chorus 2         Both: It's a quarter after one, I'm a little drunk
                          Em
                 And I need ___ you now.
                      C/G
                 Said ___ I wouldn't call but I lost all control
                          Em
                 And I need ___ you now.
                         Fmaj7sus2
                 And I don't ___ know how I can do without.

                 I just need you now.

Guitar Solo      |Am  G/B  C/G |      |Fmaj7      |Gsus4   G           |
                                                   Male: Whoa, whoa.

                 |Am  G/B  C/G |      |Fmaj7sus2  |Gsus4               |

                            Fmaj7sus2                      Am  Gsus4
Pre-Chorus 3     Both: Yes, I'd rather hurt and then feel nothing at all.

                            C/G
Chorus 3         Female: It's a quarter after one, I'm all alone
                          Em
                 And I need ___ you now.
                               C/G
                 Male: And I said ___ I wouldn't call but I'm a little drunk
                          Em
                 And I need ___ you now.
                              Fmaj7sus2
                 Both: And I don't ___ know how I can do without.
                                 C/G  Em                 C/G   Em
                 I just need you now. ___    I just need you now.
                 C/G  Em                               C/G  Em  C/G  Em*
                        Female: Oh, baby, I need you now.
```

She's Everything

Words and Music by
Brad Paisley and Wil Nance

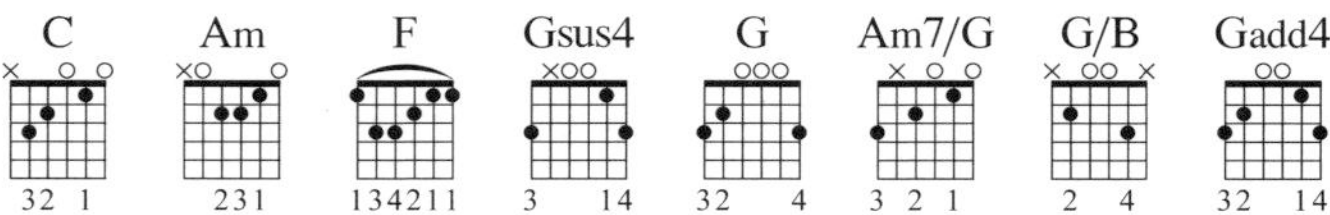

Intro |C Am |F Gsus4 G |C Am |F Gsus4 G |

Verse 1

```
      C
She's a yellow pair of runnin' shoes, a holey pair of jeans.
          Am
She looks great in cheap sunglasses, she looks great in anything.
       F
She's "I want a piece of choc'late, take me to a movie."
             G                   Am7/G
She's "I can't ___ find a thing to wear."
G
Now and then she's moody.
      C
She's a Saturn with a sunroof, with her brown hair blowin',
      Am
She's a soft place to land and a good feelin' knowin'.
      F
She's a warm conversation that I wouldn't miss for nothin'.
      G                 Am7/G
She's a fighter when she's mad
           G
And she's a    lover when she's lovin'.
```

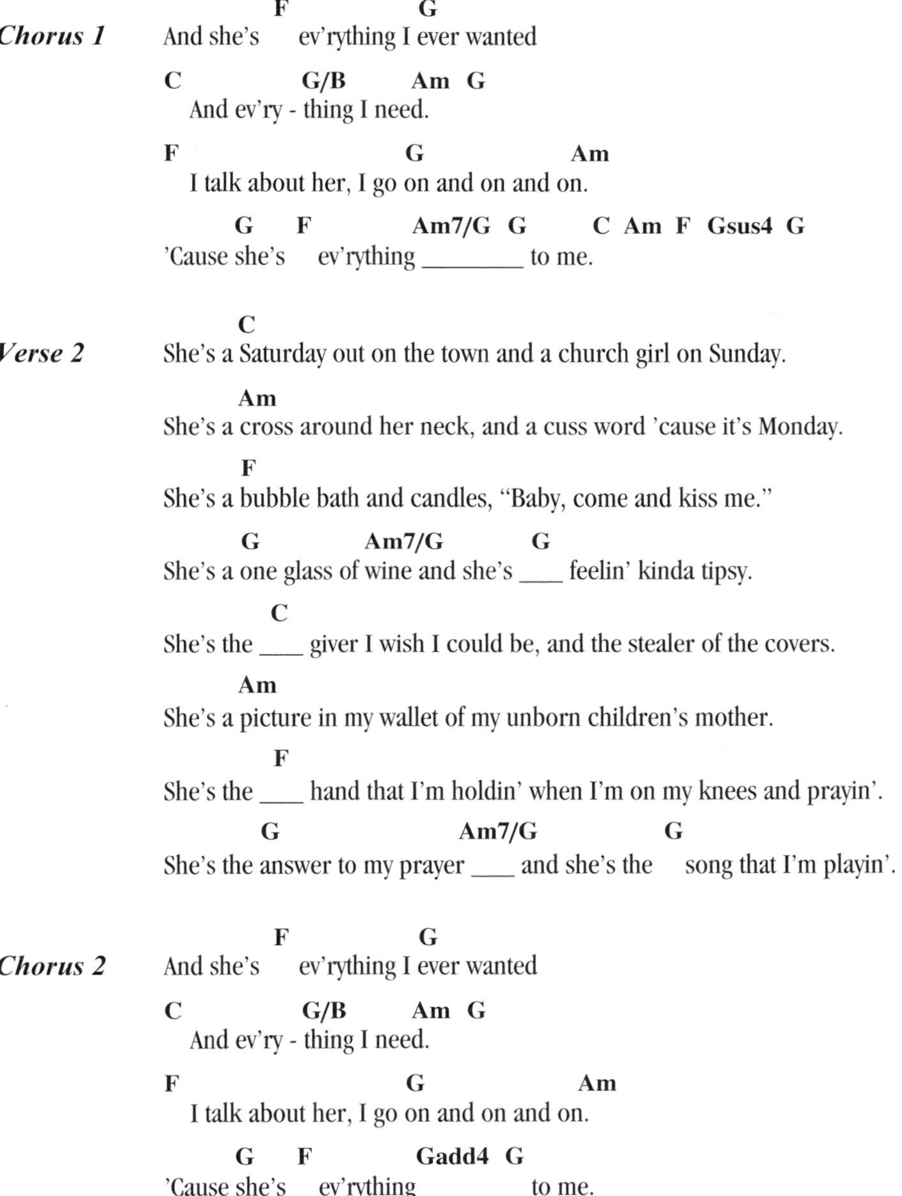

Chorus 1

F G
And she's ev'rything I ever wanted

C G/B Am G
And ev'ry - thing I need.

F G Am
I talk about her, I go on and on and on.

G F Am7/G G C Am F Gsus4 G
'Cause she's ev'rything ________ to me.

Verse 2

C
She's a Saturday out on the town and a church girl on Sunday.

Am
She's a cross around her neck, and a cuss word 'cause it's Monday.

F
She's a bubble bath and candles, "Baby, come and kiss me."

G Am7/G G
She's a one glass of wine and she's ____ feelin' kinda tipsy.

C
She's the ____ giver I wish I could be, and the stealer of the covers.

Am
She's a picture in my wallet of my unborn children's mother.

F
She's the ____ hand that I'm holdin' when I'm on my knees and prayin'.

G Am7/G G
She's the answer to my prayer ____ and she's the song that I'm playin'.

Chorus 2

F G
And she's ev'rything I ever wanted

C G/B Am G
And ev'ry - thing I need.

F G Am
I talk about her, I go on and on and on.

G F Gadd4 G
'Cause she's ev'rything ________ to me.

Guitar Solo

```
|C    Am    |F    Gsus4  G|C    Am    |F    Gsus4  G|
```

Verse 3

```
           C
She's the voice I'd love to hear someday when I'm ninety.
           Am
She's that    wooden rockin' chair I want rockin' right beside me.
F
Ev'ry day that passes I only love her more.
Gsus4                           G
   Yeah, she's the one that I'd lay down my own life for.
```

Chorus 3

```
            F           G
And she's     ev'rything I ever wanted
C              G/B       Am  G
   And ev'ry - thing I need.
F                         Gadd4  G         C  Am
   And she's ev'rything ________ to me.
              F           Gadd4  G         C  Am
Yeah, she's    ev'rything ________ to me.
F              Gadd4    G    C  Am
   Ev'rything I ever want - ed.
F                          Gadd4   G    C  Am
   And ev'rything I need.
F                          Gadd4  G        C  Am  F  Gadd4  G
   And she's ev'rything ________ to me.
```

Outro

```
||: C    Am    |F    Gsus4  G :||
```
Repeat and fade

Should've Been a Cowboy

Words and Music by
Toby Keith

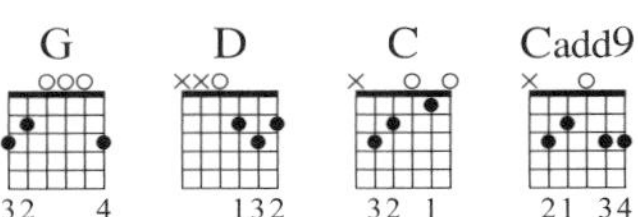

Intro

| N.C.(G) (D) | (C) (D) | (G) (D) | (C) (D) |
| G D | C D | G D | C D |

Verse 1

G D C D
I'll bet you never heard ol' Mar - shal Dillon say,

G D C D
"Miss ___ Kitty, have you ever thought of runnin' away

G D C
Or settlin' down?

D G D C
Would you marry me if I asked you twice

D G D
And begged you pretty please?"

C D G
She'd have said yes in a New York minute.

D C D G
They never tied the knot, his heart wasn't in it.

D C D
He just stole a kiss ___ as he rode away.

G D Cadd9
He never ___ hung his hat ___ up at Kitty's place.

```
                    G         D C
Chorus 1    I should've been a cowboy.

             D                    G            D   C D
            I should've learned to rope and ride,

            G          D            C          D
            Wearin' my six shooter, ridin' my pony

                 G          D C
            On a cattle drive.

            D                  G              D C D
            Stealin' the young ___ girl's hearts,

            G              D           C
            Just like Gene ___ and Roy,

            D            G          D
            Singin' those campfire songs,

            C        D                        G       D C
               Oh, I should've been a cow - boy.


                         G          D               C      D
Verse 2     I might have had a side - kick with a funny name

                           G                D               C        D
            Runnin' wild ___ through the hills chasin'     Jesse James.

               G       D                  C       D
            Or ending up on the brink ___ of danger

            G              D           C      D
            Ridin' shot - gun for the Texas Rangers.

                     G          D             C          D
            Go West ___ young man haven't you been told,

                  G            D           C             D
            Califor - nia's full of whiskey, women and gold.

                          G       D                     C      D
            Sleepin' out ___ all night beneath the desert stars

                  G             D                 Cadd2
            With a dream in my eye and a prayer ___ in my heart.
```

Chorus 2 *Repeat Chorus 1*

Guitar Solo

```
|G    D    |C    D    |G    D    |C    D    |
|G    D    |C    D    |G    D    |Cadd9     |
|          |          |
```

Chorus 3

```
                    G         D C
I should've been a cowboy.
 D                    G            D  C D
I should've learned to rope and ride,
       G          D           C        D
I'd be wearin' my six shooter, ridin' my pony
      G          D C
On a cattle drive.
D                   G               D C D
Stealin' the young ___ girl's hearts,
G                D          C
Just like Gene ___ and Roy,
D             G         D
Singin' those campfire songs,
C        D                    G        D C
   Oh, I should've been a cow - boy.
         D                    G        D C
Yeah, I should've been a cow - boy.
 D                  G      D C D
I should've been a cowboy.
```

Guitar Solo ||: G D | C D :|| ***Repeat and fade***

Somethin' Bad

Words and Music by Chris Destefano,
Brett James and Priscilla Renea

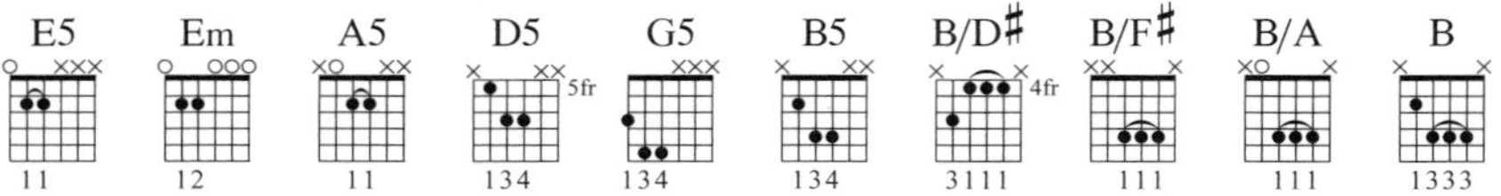

Chorus 1

N.C.
Stand on the bar, stomp your feet, start clappin'.

Got a real good feelin' somethin' bad about to happen.

Em
Oh. Oh. Oh. Oh.

Verse 1

E5
Pulled up to the church, but I got so nervous,

Had to back it on up, couldn't make it to the service.

Grab all the cash underneath my mattress,

Got a real good feelin' somethin' bad about to happen.

Em
Oh. Oh.

Verse 2

E5
Ran into a girl in a pretty white dress,

Rolled down the window, "Where are you headin' to next?"

Said, "I'm heading to the bar with my money out the mattress.

Got a real good feelin' somethin' bad about to happen.

Em
Oh. Oh.

Chorus 2

A5 **E5 D5**
Stand on the bar, stomp your feet, start clappin'.

E5 **A5**
I've got a real good feelin'

E5 A5 G5 E5
Somethin' bad about to happen.

A5
The drinks keep comin',

E5 G5 E5
Throw my head back laughin'.

B5
Wake up in the mornin', don't know what happened.

N.C.(E5)
Whoa, somethin' bad. Whoa, somethin' bad.

Verse 3

E5
Now me and that girl that I met on the street,

We're rollin' down the road, down to New Orleans.

Got a full tank of gas and the money out the mattress,

Got a real good feelin' somethin' bad about to happen.

Em
Oh. Oh.

Verse 4

E5
'Bout to tear it up down in New Orleans,

Just like a real life Thelma and Louise.

If the cops catch up, they're gonna call it kidnappin'.

Got a real good feelin' somethin' bad about to happen.

Em
Oh. Oh.

Chorus 3

Repeat Chorus 2

Outro-Chorus

A5
Stand on the bar, stomp your feet, start clappin'.

Got a real good feelin' somethin' bad about to happen.

Now, the drinks keep comin', throw my head back laughin'.

B/D♯ B/F♯ B/A B
Wake up in the mornin', don't know what happened.

N.C.(E5)
Whoa, somethin' bad. Whoa, somethin' bad.

Springsteen

Words and Music by Eric Church,
Jeffery Hyde and Ryan Tyndell

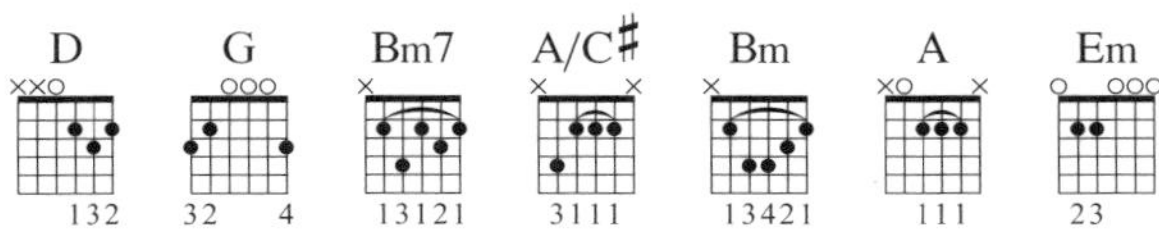

Intro | D | | G | Bm7 A/C♯ |

Verse 1

```
D
To this day when I hear that song I see you standin' there on that lawn,
G                                        Bm7                   A/C♯
Discount shades, store-bought tan,   flip-flops and cut off ___ jeans.
D
   Somewhere between that settin' sun, "I'm on fire," and "Born to Run,"
   G
You looked at me and I was done,
        Bm7                    A/C♯
But we    were just gettin' start - ed.
      D
I was singin' to you, you were singin' to me.

I was so alive, never been more free.
      G                                     Bm  A
Fired up my daddy's lighter and we sang, "Oh."
D
  Stayed there till they forced us out, and took the long way to your house.
   G                                     Bm          A
I ___ can still hear the sound of you sayin', "Don't go."
```

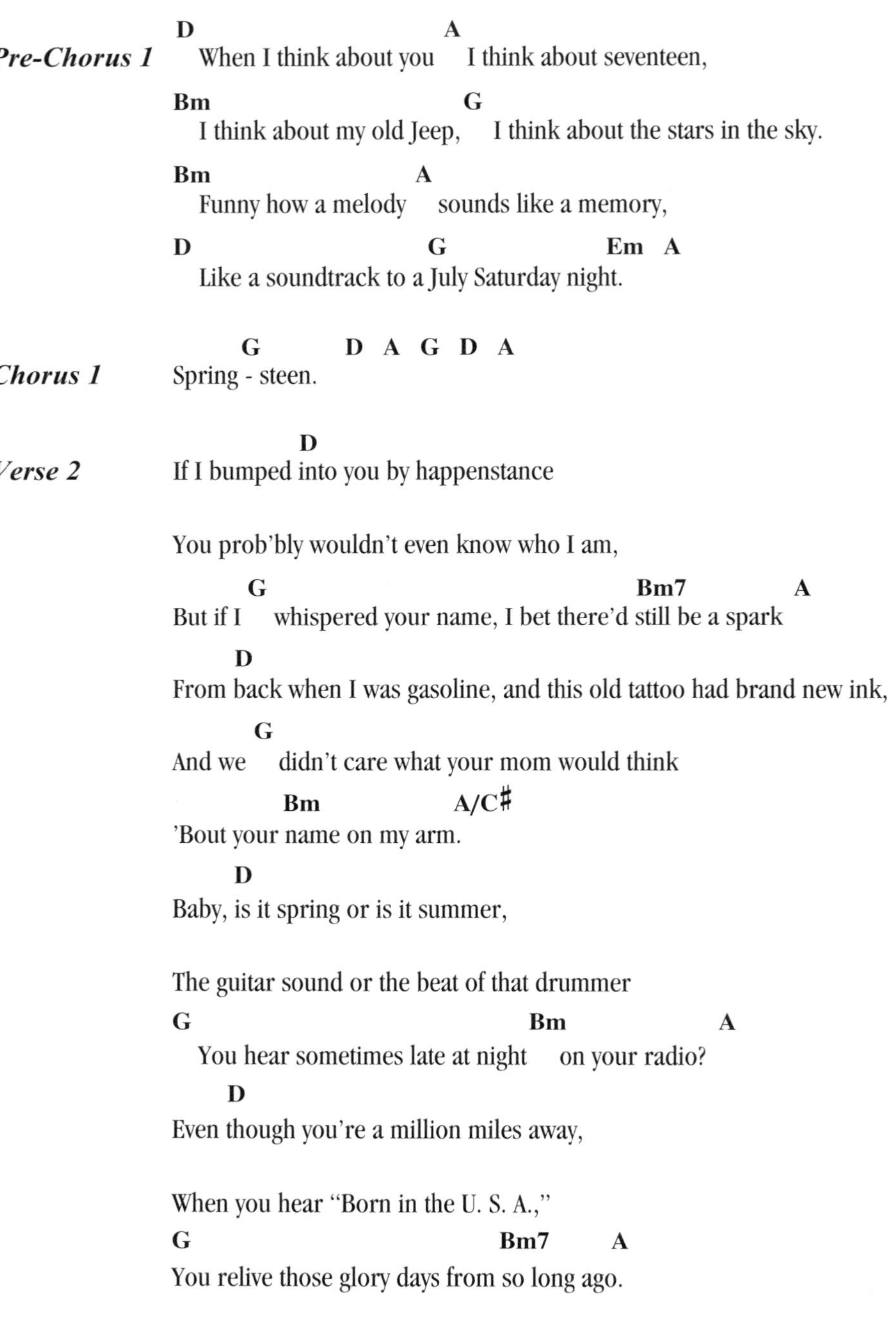

Pre-Chorus 1

D A
When I think about you I think about seventeen,

Bm G
I think about my old Jeep, I think about the stars in the sky.

Bm A
Funny how a melody sounds like a memory,

D G Em A
Like a soundtrack to a July Saturday night.

Chorus 1

G D A G D A
Spring - steen.

Verse 2

D
If I bumped into you by happenstance

You prob'bly wouldn't even know who I am,

G Bm7 A
But if I whispered your name, I bet there'd still be a spark

D
From back when I was gasoline, and this old tattoo had brand new ink,

G
And we didn't care what your mom would think

Bm A/C♯
'Bout your name on my arm.

D
Baby, is it spring or is it summer,

The guitar sound or the beat of that drummer

G Bm A
You hear sometimes late at night on your radio?

D
Even though you're a million miles away,

When you hear "Born in the U. S. A.,"

G Bm7 A
You relive those glory days from so long ago.

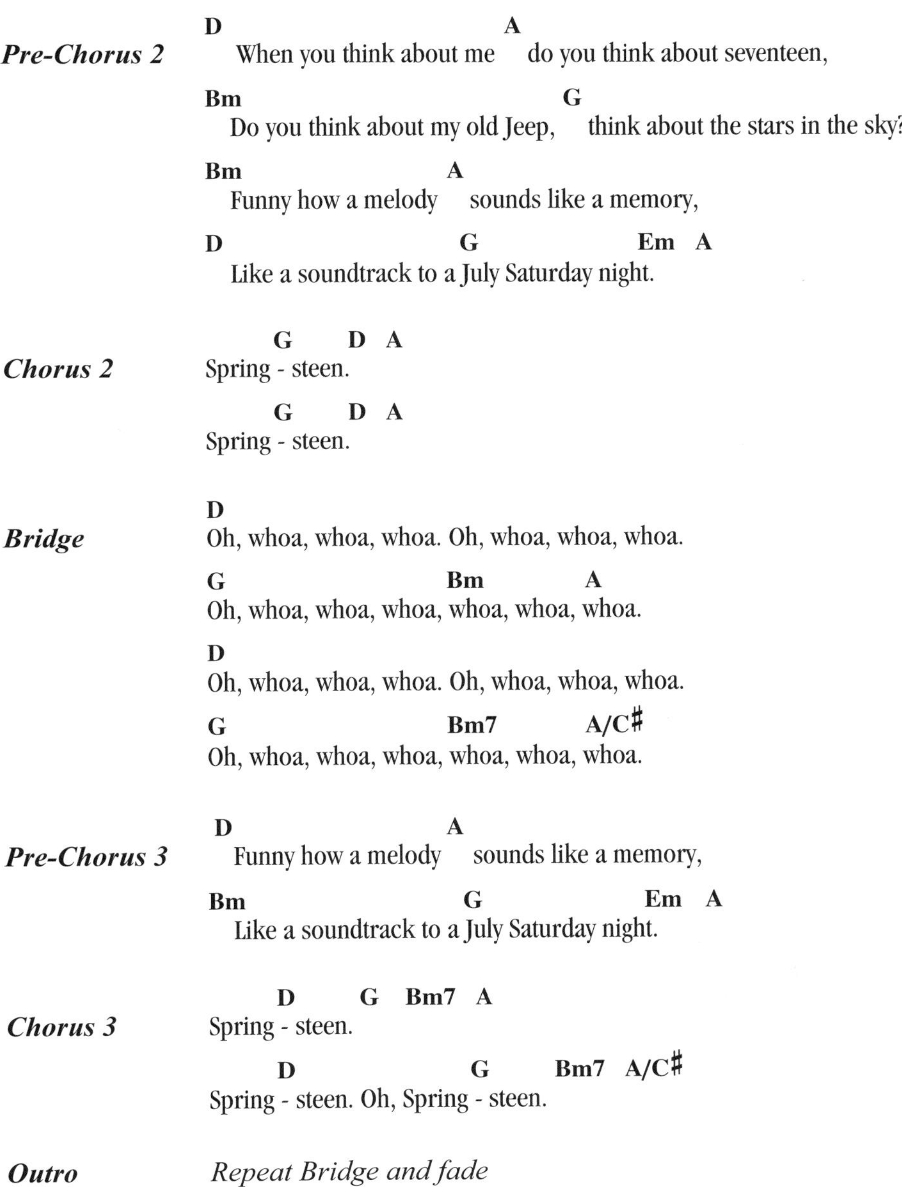

Pre-Chorus 2

D A
When you think about me do you think about seventeen,

Bm G
Do you think about my old Jeep, think about the stars in the sky?

Bm A
Funny how a melody sounds like a memory,

D G Em A
Like a soundtrack to a July Saturday night.

Chorus 2

G D A
Spring - steen.

G D A
Spring - steen.

Bridge

D
Oh, whoa, whoa, whoa. Oh, whoa, whoa, whoa.

G Bm A
Oh, whoa, whoa, whoa, whoa, whoa, whoa.

D
Oh, whoa, whoa, whoa. Oh, whoa, whoa, whoa.

G Bm7 A/C♯
Oh, whoa, whoa, whoa, whoa, whoa, whoa.

Pre-Chorus 3

D A
Funny how a melody sounds like a memory,

Bm G Em A
Like a soundtrack to a July Saturday night.

Chorus 3

D G Bm7 A
Spring - steen.

D G Bm7 A/C♯
Spring - steen. Oh, Spring - steen.

Outro

Repeat Bridge and fade

Stuck Like Glue

Words and Music by Kristian Bush,
Shy Carter, Kevin Griffin and
Jennifer Nettles

Melody:

Ab - so - lute - ly no one that knows

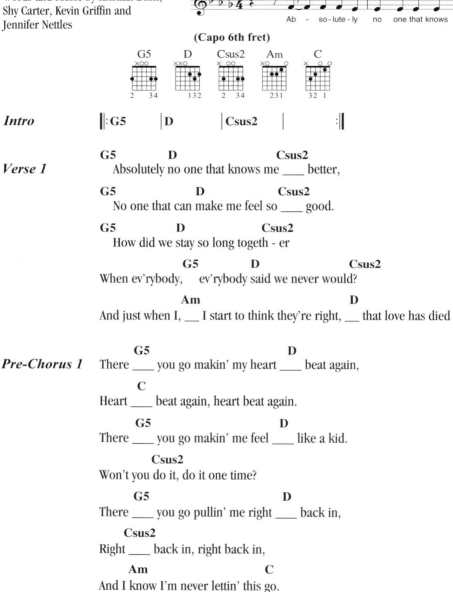

(Capo 6th fret)

G5 D Csus2 Am C

Intro ‖: **G5** | **D** | **Csus2** | :‖

Verse 1

G5 **D** **Csus2**
Absolutely no one that knows me ___ better,
G5 **D** **Csus2**
No one that can make me feel so ___ good.
G5 **D** **Csus2**
How did we stay so long togeth - er
G5 **D** **Csus2**
When ev'rybody, ev'rybody said we never would?
Am **D**
And just when I, __ I start to think they're right, __ that love has died

Pre-Chorus 1

G5 **D**
There ___ you go makin' my heart ___ beat again,
C
Heart ___ beat again, heart beat again.
G5 **D**
There ___ you go makin' me feel ___ like a kid.
Csus2
Won't you do it, do it one time?
G5 **D**
There ___ you go pullin' me right ___ back in,
Csus2
Right ___ back in, right back in,
Am **C**
And I know I'm never lettin' this go.

Chorus 1

```
D  N.C.          G5                        D
     I'm stuck on you. Wuh, oh, wuh, oh, stuck like glue.

Csus2
You and me, baby, we're stuck like glue.

G5                D
   Wuh, oh, wuh, oh, stuck like glue.

Csus2
You and me, baby, we're stuck like glue.
```

Verse 2

```
G5           D                  Csus2
   Some days ___ I don't feel like ___ tryin',

G5                    D                  Csus2
   Somedays you know ___ I wanna just give ___ up.

           G5                      D
When it does - n't matter who's right, fight about it all night,

Csus2                   G5
Had enough, you give me that look,

       D               Csus2
I'm sor - ry, baby, let's make ___ up.

Am                                 D
   You do that thing that makes me laugh.

       N.C.
And just like that,
```

Pre-Chorus 2 *Repeat Pre-Chorus 1*

Chorus 2 *Repeat Chorus 1*

N.C.

Verse 3 Wuh, oh, wuh, oh, you almost stay out,

Two stuck together from the ATL.

Wuh, oh, wuh, oh, feelin' kinda sick.

Just a spoonful o' sugar make it better real quick.

G5 **D**
I say, wuh, oh, wuh, oh, what ya gonna do with that?
Csus2 **G5**
Wuh, oh, wuh, oh, come on over here with that sugar sticky sweet stuff.
D
Come on, give me that stuff.
Csus2 **G5**
Ev'rybody wants some melodies that get stuck up in your head.
D **Csus2**
Wuh, oh, wuh, oh, up in your head.
G5
Wuh, oh, wuh, oh, up in your head.
D **Csus2**
Wuh, oh, wuh, oh, up in your head.
G5 **D**
Wuh, oh, wuh, oh, wuh, oh, wuh, oh, stuck like glue.
Csus2 **N.C.**
You and me together, say it's all I wanna do, I said...

Pre-Chorus 3

G5 D
‖: There ___ you go makin' my heart ___ beat again,

Csus2
Heart ___ beat again, heart beat again.

G5 D
There ___ you go makin' me feel ___ like a kid.

Csus2
Won't you do it, do it one time?

G5 D Csus2
There ___ you go pullin' me right ___ back in, right ___ back in,

Am C D
Right back in, and I know I'm never lettin' this go. :‖

Outro-Chorus

N.C. G5 D
I'm stuck on you. ‖: Wuh, oh, wuh, oh. Stuck like glue.

Csus2
You and me, baby, we're stuck like glue. :‖

N.C.
Wuh, oh, wuh, oh. Stuck like glue.

You and me, baby, we're stuck like glue.

Summertime

Words and Music by
Steve McEwan and Craig Wiseman

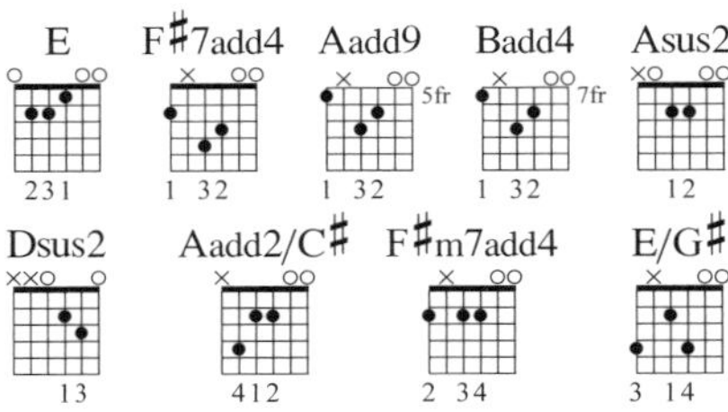

Intro | **E F♯7add4** | **Aadd9** | **E F♯7add4** | **Aadd9** |

Verse 1

E
Summertime is fin'lly here,

Aadd9
That old ballpark man is back in gear out on Forty Nine.

Man, I can see the lights.

E
School's out and the nights roll in,

Aadd9
Man, just like a long-lost friend you ain't seen in a while.

You can't help but smile.

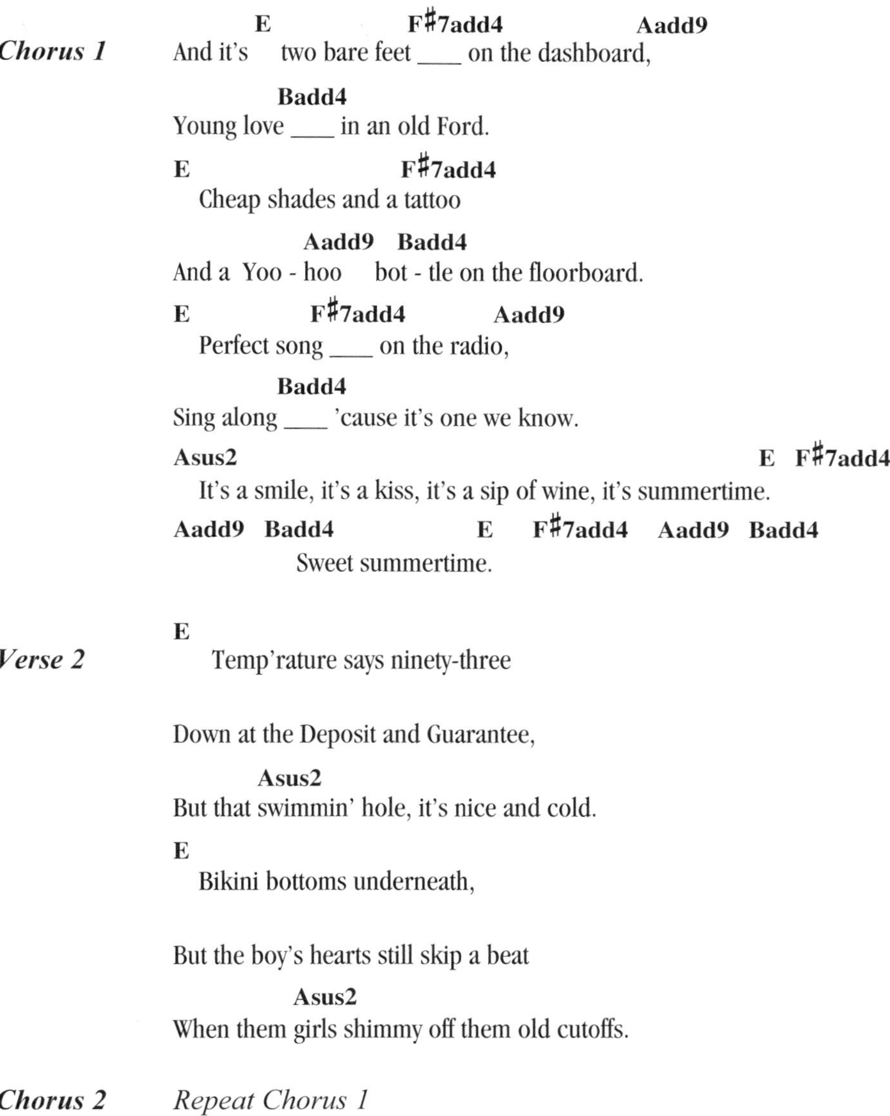

```
                E                F#7add4                 Aadd9
Chorus 1   And it's   two bare feet ___ on the dashboard,

                Badd4
           Young love ___ in an old Ford.

           E                        F#7add4
             Cheap shades and a tattoo

                     Aadd9   Badd4
           And a  Yoo - hoo    bot - tle on the floorboard.

           E               F#7add4          Aadd9
             Perfect song ___ on the radio,

                 Badd4
           Sing along ___ 'cause it's one we know.

           Asus2                                                   E   F#7add4
             It's a smile, it's a kiss, it's a sip of wine, it's summertime.

           Aadd9   Badd4               E     F#7add4    Aadd9   Badd4
                         Sweet summertime.

           E
Verse 2      Temp'rature says ninety-three

           Down at the Deposit and Guarantee,

                      Asus2
           But that swimmin' hole, it's nice and cold.

           E
             Bikini bottoms underneath,

           But the boy's hearts still skip a beat

                          Asus2
           When them girls shimmy off them old cutoffs.

Chorus 2   Repeat Chorus 1
```

Bridge

Dsus2 **Aadd2/C♯**
The more things change, the more they stay the same.

F♯m7add4 **E/G♯**
It don't matter how old ___ you are,

Aadd9
Man, you know ___ what I'm talkin' 'bout.

Badd4
Yeah, baby, when you got…

Chorus 3

E **F♯7add4** **Aadd9**
Two bare feet ___ on the dashboard,

Badd4
Young love ___ in an old Ford.

E **F♯7add4**
Cheap shades and a tattoo

Aadd9 **Badd4**
And a Yoo - hoo bottle rollin' on the floorboard.

E **F♯7add4** **Aadd9**
Perfect song ___ on the radio,

Badd4
Sing along ___ 'cause it's one we know.

Asus2 **E** **F♯7add4**
It's a smile, it's a kiss, it's a sip of wine, it's summertime.

Aadd9 **Badd4** **E** **F♯7add4** **Aadd9** **Badd4**
Sweet summertime.

Outro

‖: **E** **F♯7add4** | **Aadd9** **Badd4** :‖ ***Repeat and fade***

That Don't Impress Me Much

Words and Music by
Shania Twain and R.J. Lange

(Capo 1st fret)

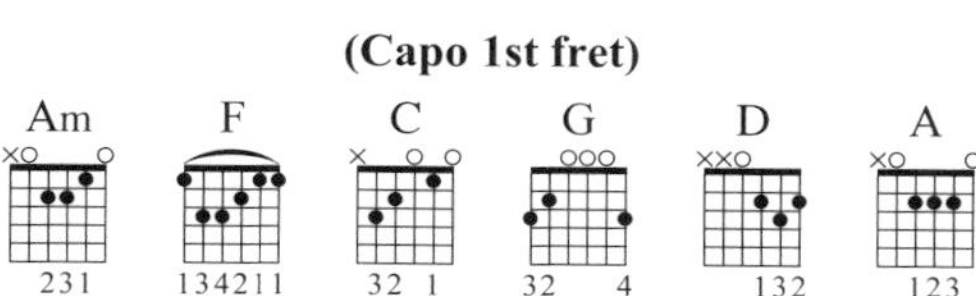

Intro | **Am F** | **C G** | **Am F** | **C G** |

Verse 1

```
    Am         F                      C       G
I've known a few guys who thought they were  pretty smart,
    Am            F       C       G
But you've got being right down ___ to an art.
    Am                   F               C       G
You think you're a gen - ius, you drive me  up the wall.
          Am        F       C       G
You're a regular o - riginal, a  know it all.
D  A      G
Oh, oh, you think you're special.
D  A                 G
Oh, oh, you think you're something else.
          N.C.
Spoken:   Okay, so you're a rocket scientist.
```

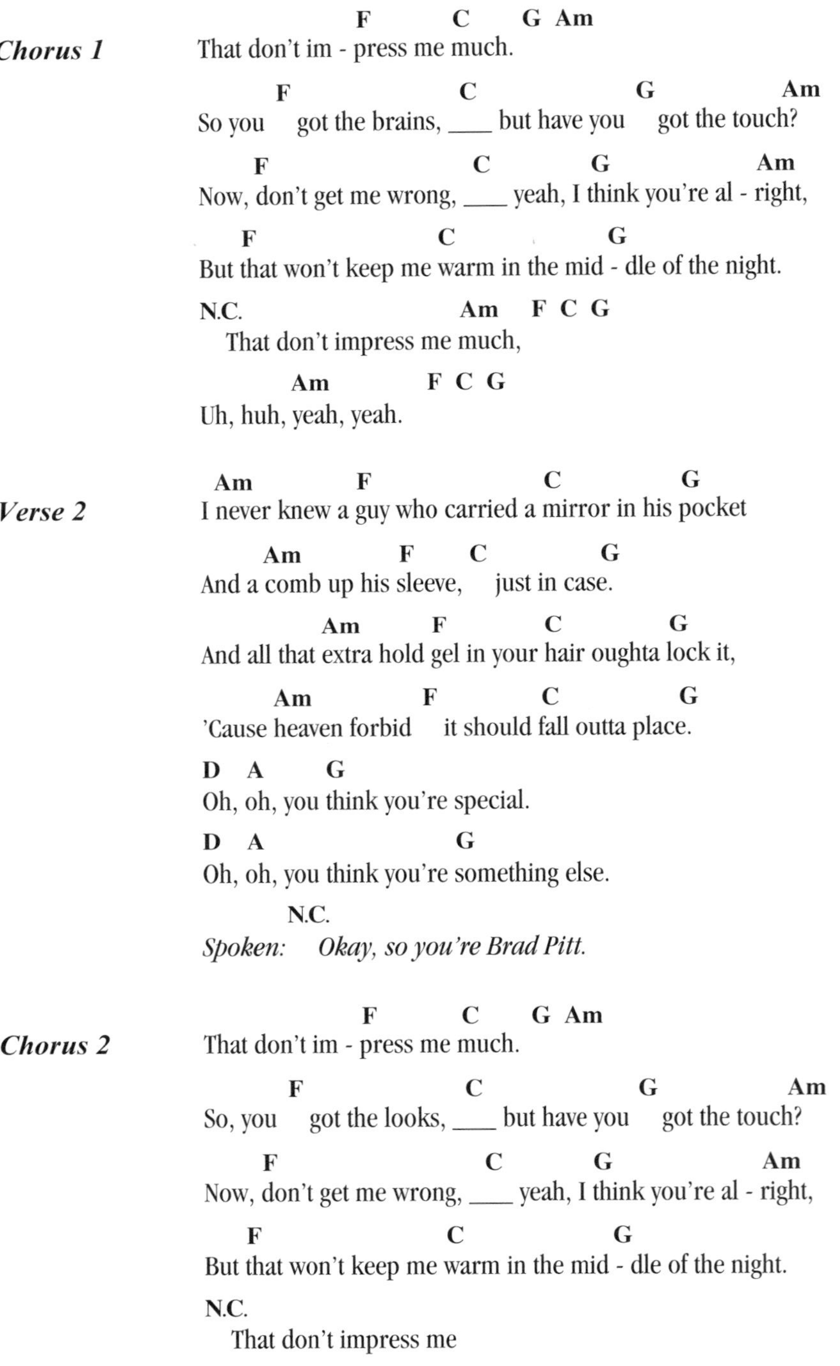

```
                      F          C        G  Am
Chorus 1     That don't im - press me much.

                  F                  C                  G              Am
             So you    got the brains, ___ but have you    got the touch?

                 F                     C           G                Am
             Now, don't get me wrong, ___ yeah, I think you're al - right,

                F                  C                  G
             But that won't keep me warm in the mid - dle of the night.

             N.C.                       Am     F  C  G
                That don't impress me much,

                       Am             F  C  G
             Uh, huh, yeah, yeah.

               Am            F                      C               G
Verse 2      I never knew a guy who carried a mirror in his pocket

                  Am          F       C              G
             And a comb up his sleeve,    just in case.

                        Am        F            C              G
             And all that extra hold gel in your hair oughta lock it,

                    Am            F           C             G
             'Cause heaven forbid    it should fall outta place.

             D   A      G
             Oh, oh, you think you're special.
             D   A                   G
             Oh, oh, you think you're something else.

                         N.C.
             Spoken:    Okay, so you're Brad Pitt.

                      F          C        G  Am
Chorus 2     That don't im - press me much.

                    F                  C                  G              Am
             So, you    got the looks, ___ but have you    got the touch?

                 F                     C           G                Am
             Now, don't get me wrong, ___ yeah, I think you're al - right,

                F                  C                  G
             But that won't keep me warm in the mid - dle of the night.

             N.C.
                That don't impress me
```

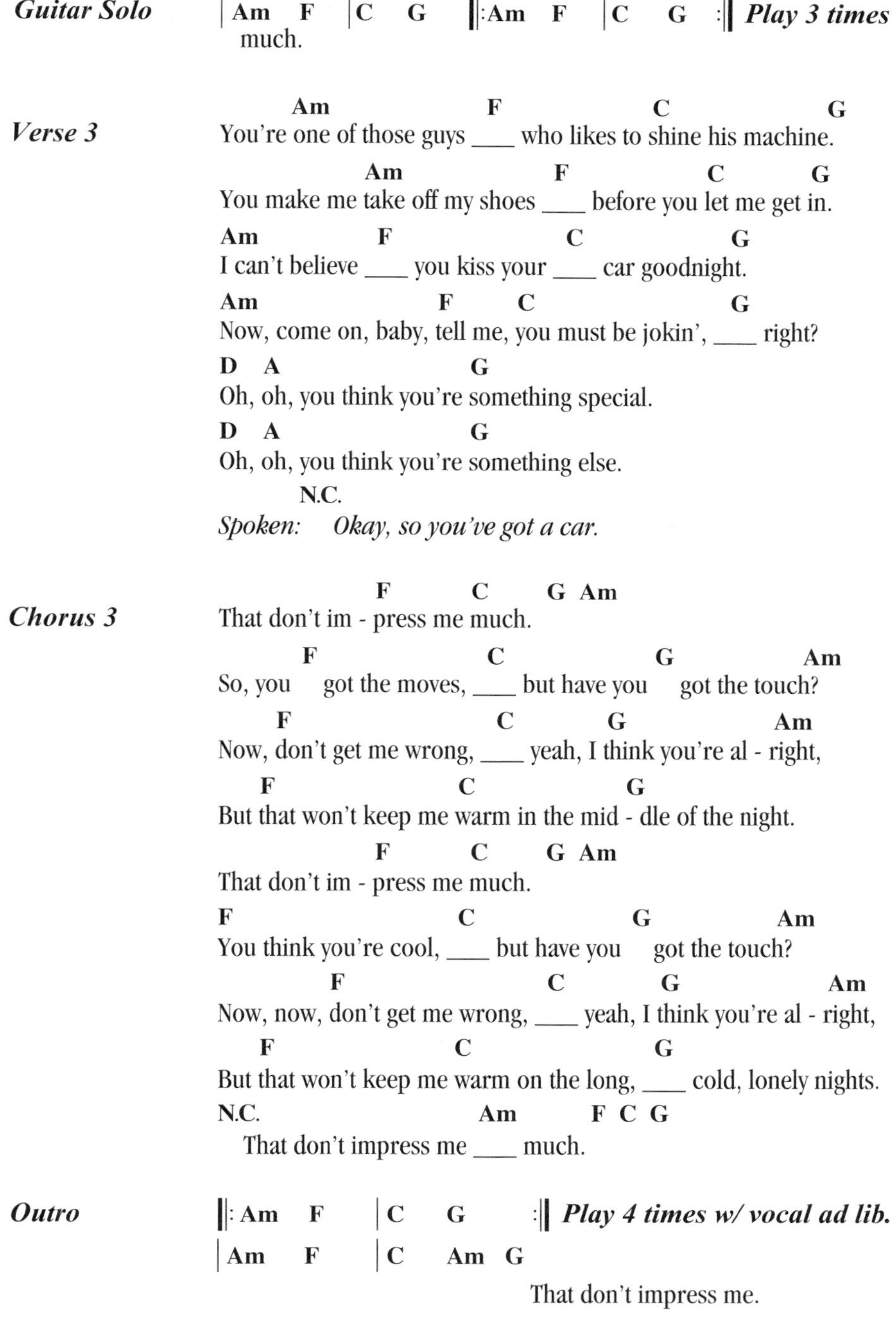

Guitar Solo | Am F | C G ||: Am F | C G :|| ***Play 3 times***
much.

Verse 3
Am F C G
You're one of those guys ___ who likes to shine his machine.
Am F C G
You make me take off my shoes ___ before you let me get in.
Am F C G
I can't believe ___ you kiss your ___ car goodnight.
Am F C G
Now, come on, baby, tell me, you must be jokin', ___ right?
D A G
Oh, oh, you think you're something special.
D A G
Oh, oh, you think you're something else.
N.C.
Spoken: Okay, so you've got a car.

Chorus 3
F C G Am
That don't im - press me much.
F C G Am
So, you got the moves, ___ but have you got the touch?
F C G Am
Now, don't get me wrong, ___ yeah, I think you're al - right,
F C G
But that won't keep me warm in the mid - dle of the night.
F C G Am
That don't im - press me much.
F C G Am
You think you're cool, ___ but have you got the touch?
F C G Am
Now, now, don't get me wrong, ___ yeah, I think you're al - right,
F C G
But that won't keep me warm on the long, ___ cold, lonely nights.
N.C. Am F C G
That don't impress me ___ much.

Outro ||: Am F | C G :|| ***Play 4 times w/ vocal ad lib.***
| Am F | C Am G
That don't impress me.

Three Wooden Crosses

Words and Music by
Kim Williams and Doug Johnson

Melody:

A farm - er and _ a teach - er,

(Capo 1st fret)

C C/B Am7 C/G Am F G7 Dm Gsus4

Intro | C | C/B | Am7 | C/G |

Verse 1

```
 C                    C/B  Am                  C/G
A farmer and a teacher,    a hooker and a preacher,
F                         C               G
Ridin' on a midnight bus, bound for Mexico.
        C                  C/B        Am
One was headed for vacation,   one for higher education
    F                       G7         C
And two of them were search - in' for lost souls.
    Dm                           G
That driver never ever saw the stop ____ sign
    Dm                                  Gsus4  G
And eighteen wheelers can't stop on a dime.
```

Chorus 1

```
          C               C/B
There are    three wooden cross - es
              Am             C/G
On the right ____ side of the high - way.
F                              C               G
   Why there's not four of them heaven only knows.
             C              C/B
I guess it's    not what you take
                Am                 C/G
When you leave ____ this world behind ____ you,
    F                  G7               C
It's what you leave behind ____ you when you go.
```

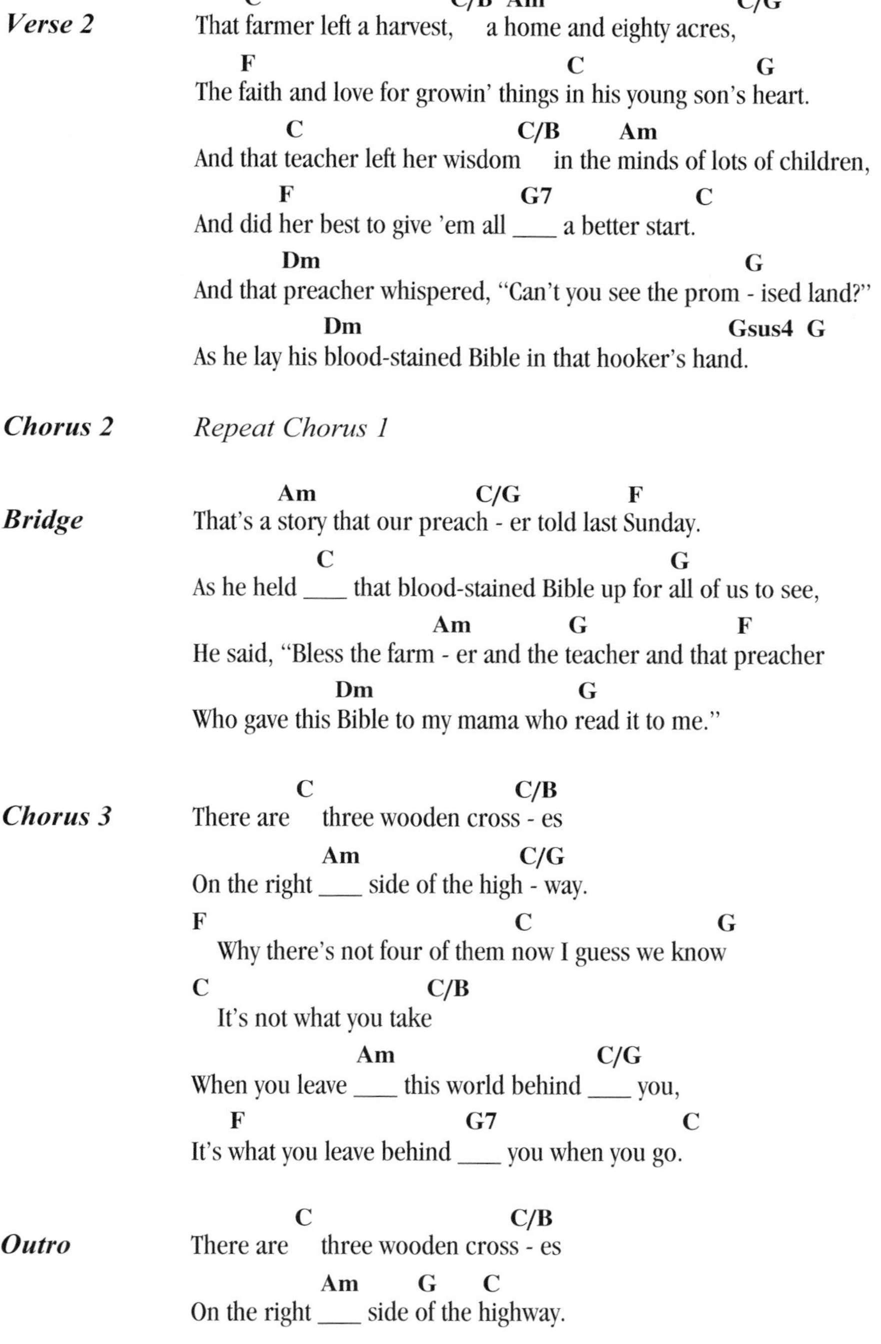

```
               C                       C/B  Am                   C/G
Verse 2        That farmer left a harvest,     a home and eighty acres,
                F                                C               G
               The faith and love for growin' things in his young son's heart.
                  C                          C/B       Am
               And that teacher left her wisdom     in the minds of lots of children,
                   F                           G7             C
               And did her best to give 'em all ___ a better start.
                   Dm                                                G
               And that preacher whispered, "Can't you see the prom - ised land?"
                      Dm                                         Gsus4  G
               As he lay his blood-stained Bible in that hooker's hand.

Chorus 2       Repeat Chorus 1

                   Am               C/G            F
Bridge         That's a story that our preach - er told last Sunday.
                      C                                     G
               As he held ___ that blood-stained Bible up for all of us to see,
                                  Am          G              F
               He said, "Bless the farm - er and the teacher and that preacher
                         Dm                 G
               Who gave this Bible to my mama who read it to me."

                   C                  C/B
Chorus 3       There are     three wooden cross - es
                         Am                C/G
               On the right ___ side of the high - way.
               F                       C                   G
                  Why there's not four of them now I guess we know
               C                 C/B
                  It's not what you take
                           Am                   C/G
               When you leave ___ this world behind ___ you,
                 F                      G7                  C
               It's what you leave behind ___ you when you go.

                   C                  C/B
Outro          There are     three wooden cross - es
                         Am       G     C
               On the right ___ side of the highway.
```

Wanted

Words and Music by
Hunter Hayes and Troy Verges

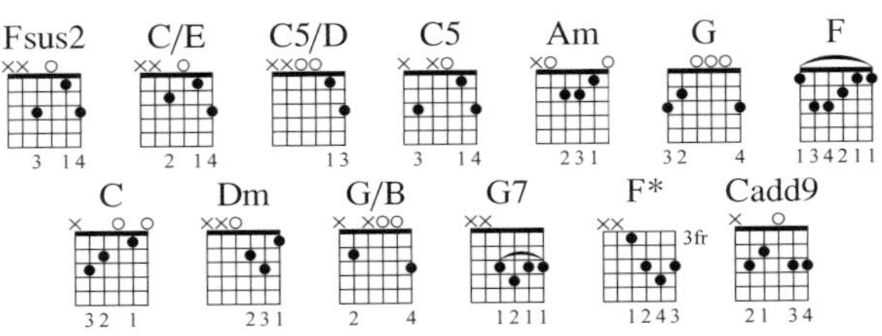

Intro ‖: Fsus2 C/E | C5/D C/E :‖

Verse 1

Fsus2 C/E C5/D C/E
You know I'd fall apart with - out you.

Fsus2 C/E C5/D C5
I don't know how you do what you do.

Fsus2 C/E C/D C/E
'Cause ev'rything that don't make sense a - bout me

Fsus2 C/E C/D C5
Makes sense when I'm with you.

Fsus2 C/E C5/D C/E
Like ev'rything that's green, girl I need ___ you.

Fsus2 C/E C5/D C5
But it's more than one and one makes ___ two.

Fsus2 C/E C5/D C/E
Put aside the math and the log - ic of it

Fsus2 C/E C5/D C5
You gotta know you want it too.

Chorus 1

Am G
'Cause I wanna wrap you ___ up,

F C
Wanna kiss your ___ lips.

Am G F C
I, I wan - na make you feel want - ed.

Am G
And I wanna call you ___ mine.

F C Am
Wanna hold your ___ hand forev - er

G F C
And never ___ let you forget ___ it,

Am G Fsus2 C/E C5/D C5
Yeah, I, I wanna ___ make you feel want - ed.

Verse 2

Fsus2 C/E C5/D C/E
Well, anyone can tell ya you're pret - ty.

Fsus2 C/E C5/D C5
And you get that all the time, I know you do.

Fsus2 C/E C5/D C/E
But your beauty's ___ deeper than the makeup.

Fsus2 C/E C5/D C5
And I wanna ___ show you what I see to - night.

Chorus 2

Am G
When I wrap you ___ up,

F C
When I kiss your ___ lips.

Am G F C
I, I wan - na make you feel want - ed.

Am G
And I wanna call you ___ mine.

F C Am
Wanna hold your ___ hand forev - er

G F C
And never ___ let you forget ___ it,

Am G F
'Cause baby, I, ___ I wan - na make you feel want - ed.

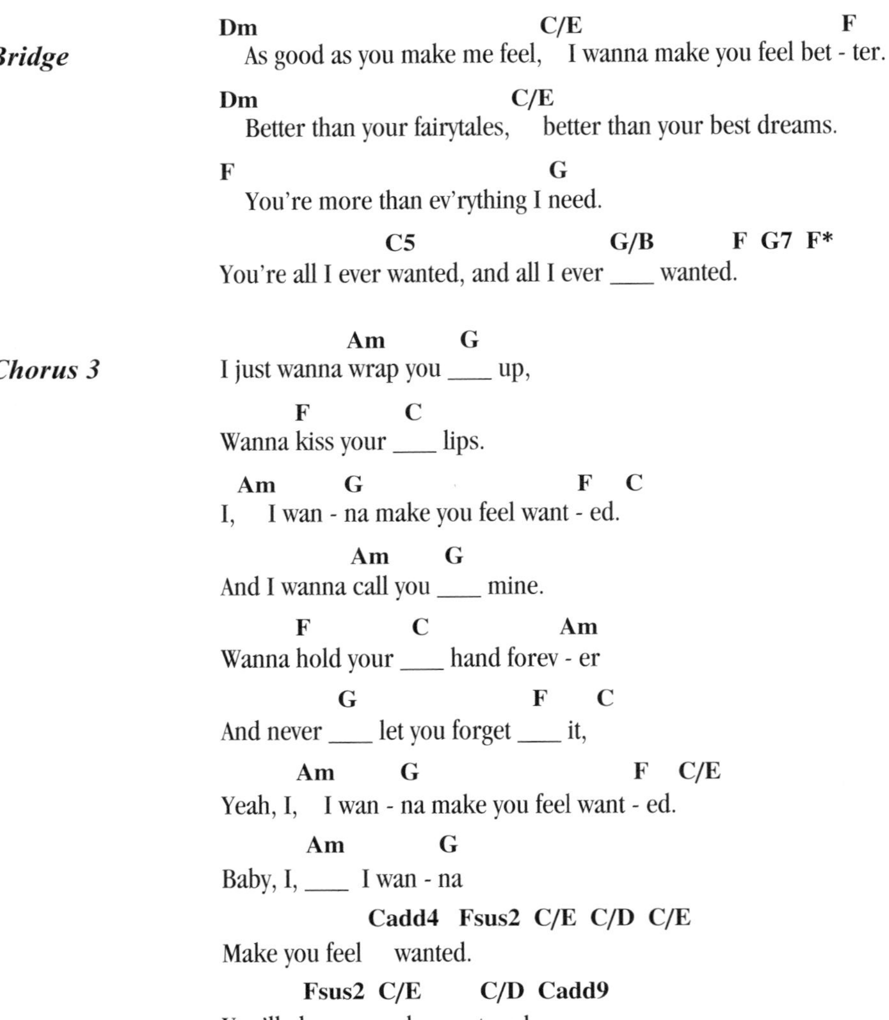

Bridge

Dm C/E F
As good as you make me feel, I wanna make you feel bet - ter.

Dm C/E
Better than your fairytales, better than your best dreams.

F G
You're more than ev'rything I need.

C5 G/B F G7 F*
You're all I ever wanted, and all I ever ___ wanted.

Chorus 3

Am G
I just wanna wrap you ___ up,

F C
Wanna kiss your ___ lips.

Am G F C
I, I wan - na make you feel want - ed.

Am G
And I wanna call you ___ mine.

F C Am
Wanna hold your ___ hand forev - er

G F C
And never ___ let you forget ___ it,

Am G F C/E
Yeah, I, I wan - na make you feel want - ed.

Am G
Baby, I, ___ I wan - na

Cadd4 Fsus2 C/E C/D C/E
Make you feel wanted.

Fsus2 C/E C/D Cadd9
You'll al - ways be want - ed.

Your Man

Words and Music by Jace Everett,
Chris DuBois and Chris Stapleton

(Capo 2nd fret)

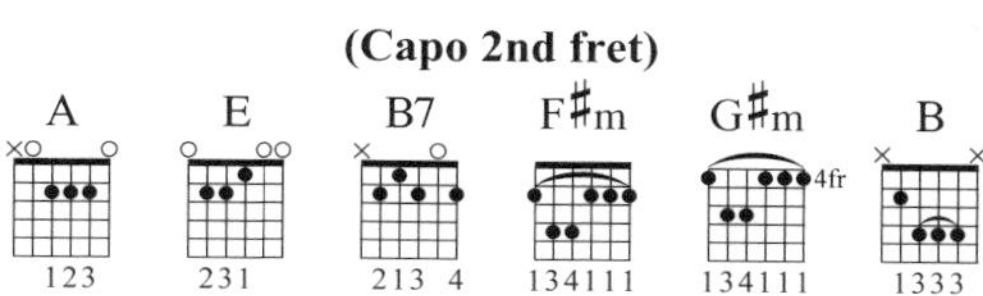

Intro

| N.C. | A | | E |
| | B7 | | E |

Chorus 1

```
E  N.C.                                      A
   Baby, lock the door and turn the lights down low
                                        E
And put some music on that's soft and slow.
                                 B7
Baby, we ain't got no place to go.
                                  E
I hope you understand
N.C.                              A
I've been thinkin' 'bout this all day long.
                              E
Never felt a feelin' quite this strong.
                                      B7
I can't believe how much it turns me on
                              E
Just to be your man.
```

Verse 1

F♯m
There's no hurry, don't you worry.

E
We can take our time.

F♯m **G♯m**
Come a little closer, let's go over

A **B**
What I had in mind.

Chorus 2

N.C. **A**
Baby, lock the door and turn the lights down low

E
And put some music on that's soft and slow.

B7
Baby, we ain't got no place to go.

E
I hope you understand

N.C. **A**
I've been thinkin' 'bout this all day long.

E
Never felt a feelin' quite this strong.

B7
I can't believe how much it turns me on

E
Just to be your man.

Guitar Solo

| **A** | | **E** | |
| **B7** | | **E** | |

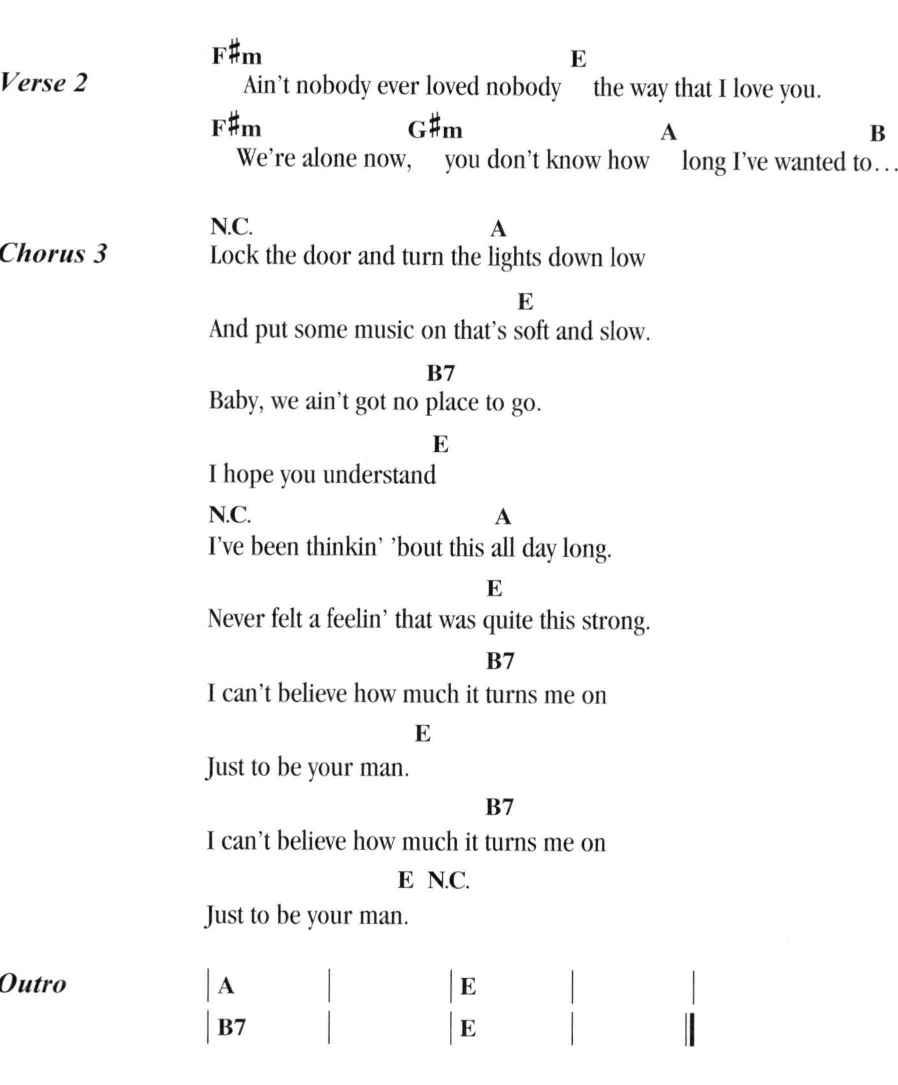

Verse 2

```
F#m                                E
   Ain't nobody ever loved nobody    the way that I love you.
F#m                 G#m                     A                  B
   We're alone now,    you don't know how    long I've wanted to...
```

Chorus 3

```
N.C.                          A
Lock the door and turn the lights down low
                                  E
And put some music on that's soft and slow.
                          B7
Baby, we ain't got no place to go.
                          E
I hope you understand
N.C.                         A
I've been thinkin' 'bout this all day long.
                               E
Never felt a feelin' that was quite this strong.
                               B7
I can't believe how much it turns me on
                        E
Just to be your man.
                               B7
I can't believe how much it turns me on
                       E  N.C.
Just to be your man.
```

Outro

```
| A        |          | E        |          |
| B7       |          | E        |          ||
```

What About Now

Words and Music by
Ron Harbin, Anthony Smith
and Aaron Barker

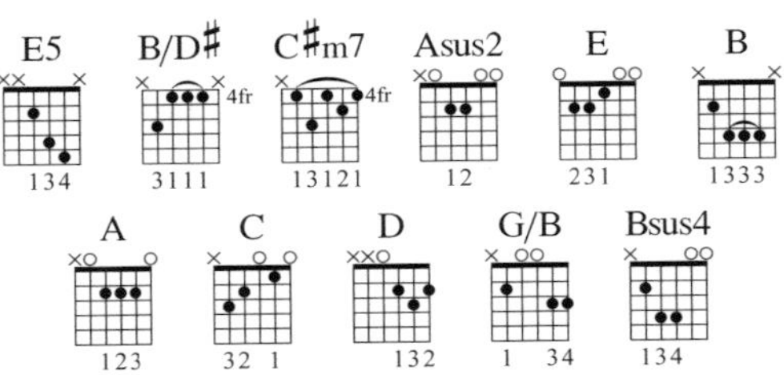

Intro

| E5 | B/D♯ | C♯m7 | Asus2 |
| E | B | C♯m7 | Asus2 |

Verse 1

```
          E
The sign ___ in the window said for sale or trade
              B
On the last ___ remaining dinosaur Detroit made.
    A
Sev - en hundred dollars was a heck of a deal
              B
For a four ___ hundred horse power jukebox on wheels.
```

Verse 2

```
A                E
And that road ___ rolls out like a welcome mat.
                B
I don't know ___ where it goes, but it beats where we're at.
      A
We al - ways said someday, somehow,
               B
We're gonna get away, gonna blow this town.
```

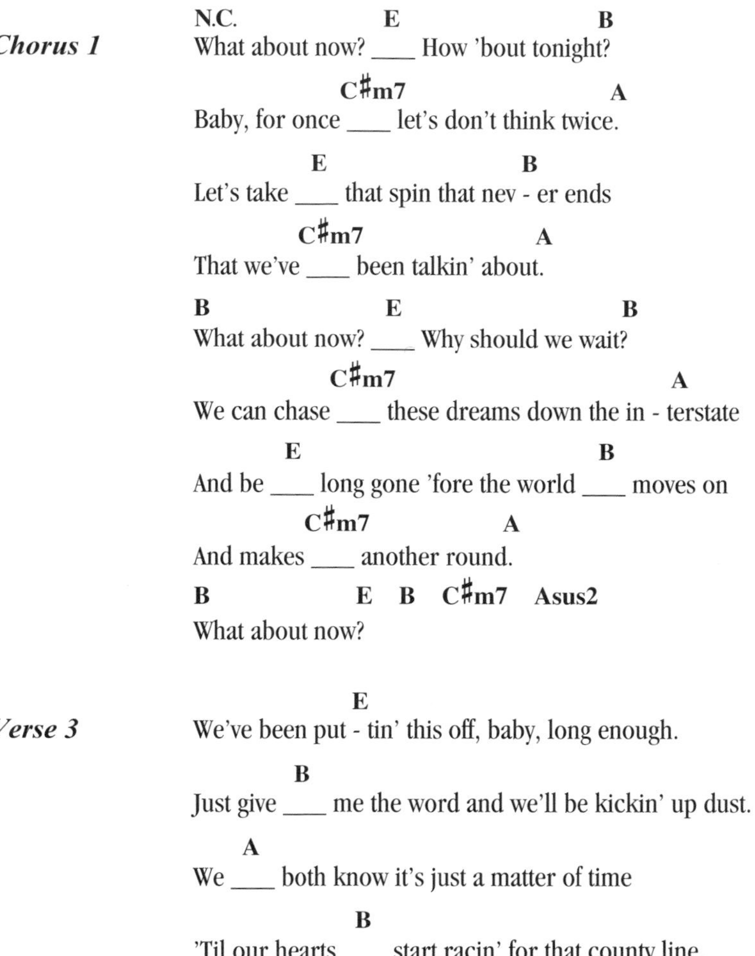

```
               N.C.                E                        B
*Chorus 1*     What about now? ___ How 'bout tonight?

                                C#m7                        A
               Baby, for once ___ let's don't think twice.

                           E                      B
               Let's take ___ that spin that nev - er ends

                             C#m7                 A
               That we've ___ been talkin' about.

               B                   E                          B
               What about now? ___ Why should we wait?

                                 C#m7                              A
               We can chase ___ these dreams down the in - terstate

                          E                                  B
               And be ___ long gone 'fore the world ___ moves on

                              C#m7              A
               And makes ___ another round.

               B                 E    B    C#m7    Asus2
               What about now?


                                E
*Verse 3*      We've been put - tin' this off, baby, long enough.

                          B
               Just give ___ me the word and we'll be kickin' up dust.

                      A
               We ___ both know it's just a matter of time

                                  B
               'Til our hearts ___ start racin' for that county line.
```

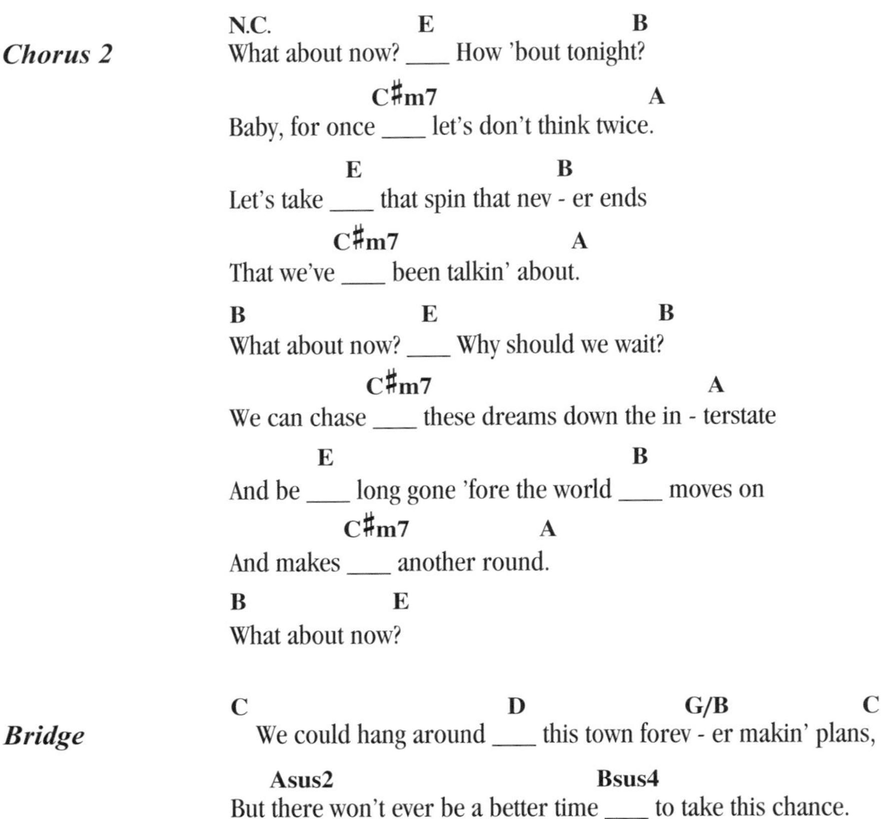

Chorus 2

N.C. E B
What about now? ___ How 'bout tonight?

C♯m7 A
Baby, for once ___ let's don't think twice.

E B
Let's take ___ that spin that nev - er ends

C♯m7 A
That we've ___ been talkin' about.

B E B
What about now? ___ Why should we wait?

C♯m7 A
We can chase ___ these dreams down the in - terstate

E B
And be ___ long gone 'fore the world ___ moves on

C♯m7 A
And makes ___ another round.

B E
What about now?

Bridge

C D G/B C
We could hang around ___ this town forev - er makin' plans,

Asus2 Bsus4
But there won't ever be a better time ___ to take this chance.

Chorus 3

```
                    E                        B/D#
What about now? ___ How 'bout tonight?
                C#m7                        Asus2
Baby, for once ___ let's don't think twice.
           E                         B
Let's take ___ that spin that nev - er ends
        C#m7                     A
That we've ___ been talkin' about.
N.C.                 E                        B
What about now? ___Why should we wait?
              C#m7                                A
We can chase ___ these dreams down the in - terstate
        E                                B
And be ___ long gone 'fore the world ___ moves on
          C#m7                A
And makes ___ another round.
B                  E    B   C#m7  A
What about now?              Oh.
                  E    B   C#m7   A  B    E
What about now?
```

. 100 – B.B. KING .... 00700466 / $16.99
. 101 – SONGS FOR BEGINNERS .... 00701917 / $14.99
. 102 – CLASSIC PUNK .... 00700769 / $14.99
. 104 – DUANE ALLMAN .... 00700846 / $16.99
. 106 – WEEZER .... 00700958 / $14.99
. 107 – CREAM .... 00701069 / $16.99
. 108 – THE WHO .... 00701053 / $16.99
. 109 – STEVE MILLER .... 00701054 / $14.99
. 110 – SLIDE GUITAR HITS .... 00701055 / $16.99
. 111 – JOHN MELLENCAMP .... 00701056 / $14.99
. 112 – QUEEN .... 00701052 / $16.99
. 113 – JIM CROCE .... 00701058 / $15.99
. 114 – BON JOVI .... 00701060 / $14.99
. 115 – JOHNNY CASH .... 00701070 / $16.99
. 116 – THE VENTURES .... 00701124 / $14.99
. 117 – BRAD PAISLEY 00701224/ $16.99
. 118 – ERIC JOHNSON .... 00701353 / $16.99
. 119 – AC/DC CLASSICS .... 00701356 / $17.99
. 120 – PROGRESSIVE ROCK .... 00701457 / $14.99
. 121 – U2 .... 00701508 / $16.99
. 122 – CROSBY, STILLS & NASH .. 00701610 / $16.99
. 123 – LENNON & MCCARTNEY ACOUSTIC .... 00701614 / $16.99
. 125 – JEFF BECK .... 00701687 / $16.99
. 126 – BOB MARLEY .... 00701701 / $16.99
. 127 – 1970s ROCK .... 00701739 / $14.99
. 128 – 1960s ROCK .... 00701740 / $14.99
. 129 – MEGADETH .... 00701741 / $16.99
. 131 – 1990s ROCK .... 00701743 / $14.99
. 132 – COUNTRY ROCK .... 00701757 / $15.99
. 133 – TAYLOR SWIFT .... 00701894 / $16.99
. 134 – AVENGED SEVENFOLD .... 00701906 / $16.99
. 136 – GUITAR THEMES .... 00701922 / $14.99
. 137 – IRISH TUNES .... 00701966 / $15.99
. 138 – BLUEGRASS CLASSICS .... 00701967 / $14.99
. 139 – GARY MOORE .... 00702370 / $16.99
. 140 – MORE STEVIE RAY VAUGHAN .... 00702396 / $17.99
. 141 – ACOUSTIC HITS .... 00702401 / $16.99
. 142 – KINGS OF LEON .... 00702418 / $16.99
. 144 – DJANGO REINHARDT .... 00702531 / $16.99

VOL. 145 – DEF LEPPARD .... 00702532 / $16.99
VOL. 147 – SIMON & GARFUNKEL .... 14041591 / $16.99
VOL. 148 – BOB DYLAN .... 14041592 / $16.99
VOL. 149 – AC/DC HITS .... 14041593 / $17.99
VOL. 150 – ZAKK WYLDE .... 02501717 / $16.99
VOL. 152 – JOE BONAMASSA .... 02501751 / $19.99
VOL. 153 – RED HOT CHILI PEPPERS ... 00702990 / $19.99
VOL. 155 – ERIC CLAPTON – FROM THE ALBUM UNPLUGGED .... 00703085 / $16.99
VOL. 156 – SLAYER .... 00703770 / $17.99
VOL. 157 – FLEETWOOD MAC .... 00101382 / $16.99
VOL. 158 – ULTIMATE CHRISTMAS .... 00101889 / $14.99
VOL. 160 – T-BONE WALKER 00102641/ $16.99
VOL. 161 – THE EAGLES – ACOUSTIC ... 00102659 / $17.99
VOL. 162 – THE EAGLES HITS .... 00102667 / $17.99
VOL. 163 – PANTERA .... 00103036 / $17.99
VOL. 166 – MODERN BLUES .... 00700764 / $16.99
VOL. 167 – DREAM THEATER .... 00111938 / $24.99
VOL. 168 – KISS .... 00113421 / $16.99
VOL. 169 – TAYLOR SWIFT .... 00115982 / $16.99
VOL. 170 – THREE DAYS GRACE .... 00117337 / $16.99
VOL. 171 – JAMES BROWN .... 00117420 / $16.99
VOL. 172 – THE DOOBIE BROTHERS .... 00119670 / $16.99
VOL. 173 – TRANS-SIBERIAN ORCHESTRA .... 00119907 / $19.99
VOL. 174 – SCORPIONS .... 00122119 / $16.99
VOL. 176 – BLUES BREAKERS WITH JOHN MAYALL & ERIC CLAPTON .... 00122132 / $19.99
VOL. 177 – ALBERT KING .... 00123271 / $16.99
VOL. 178 – JASON MRAZ .... 00124165 / $17.99
VOL. 179 – RAMONES .... 00127073 / $16.99
VOL. 180 – BRUNO MARS .... 00129706 / $16.99
VOL. 181 – JACK JOHNSON .... 00129854 / $16.99

Complete series list and song lists available online.

Prices, contents, and availability subject to change without notice.

www.halleonard.com

0615

John Denver
50 favorites: Annie's Song • Leaving on a Jet Plane • Rocky Mountain High • Take Me Home, Country Roads • Thank God I'm a Country Boy • and more.
02501697 ....$14.99

Neil Diamond
50 songs: America • Cherry, Cherry • Cracklin' Rosie • Forever in Blue Jeans • I Am...I Said • Love on the Rocks • Song Sung Blue • Sweet Caroline • and dozens more!
00700606 ....$14.99

Disney
56 super Disney songs: Be Our Guest • Friend like Me • Hakuna Matata • It's a Small World • Under the Sea • A Whole New World • Zip-A-Dee-Doo-Dah • and more!
00701071 ....$14.99

The Best of Bob Dylan
70 Dylan classics: Blowin' in the Wind • Forever Young • Hurricane • It Ain't Me Babe • Just like a Woman • Lay Lady Lay • Like a Rolling Stone • and more.
14037617 ....$17.99

Eagles
40 familiar songs: Already Gone • Best of My Love • Desperado • Hotel California • Life in the Fast Lane • Peaceful Easy Feeling • Witchy Woman • more.
00122917 ....$16.99

Folk Pop Rock
80 songs: American Pie • Dust in the Wind • Me and Bobby McGee • Somebody to Love • Time in a Bottle • and more.
00699651 ....$14.95

Folksongs
80 folk favorites: Aura Lee • Camptown Races • Danny Boy • Man of Constant Sorrow • Nobody Knows the Trouble I've Seen • and more.
00699541 ....$12.95

40 Easy Strumming Songs
Features 40 songs: Cat's in the Cradle • Daughter • Hey, Soul Sister • Homeward Bound • Take It Easy • Wild Horses • and more.
00115972 ....$14.99

Four Chord Songs
40 hit songs: Blowin' in the Wind • I Saw Her Standing There • Should I Stay or Should I Go • Stand by Me • Turn the Page • Wonderful Tonight • and more.
00701611 ....$12.99

Glee
50+ hits: Bad Romance • Beautiful • Dancing with Myself • Don't Stop Believin' • Imagine • Rehab • Teenage Dream • True Colors • and dozens more.
00702501 ....$14.99

Gospel Hymns
80 hymns: Amazing Grace • Give Me That Old Time Religion • I Love to Tell the Story • Shall We Gather at the River? • Wondrous Love • and more.
00700463 ....$14.99

Grand Ole Opry®
80 great songs: Abilene • Act Naturally • Country Boy • Crazy • Friends in Low Places • He Stopped Loving Her Today • Wings of a Dove • dozens more!
00699885 ....$16.95

Green Day
34 faves: American Idiot • Basket Case • Boulevard of Broken Dreams • Good Riddance (Time of Your Life) • 21 Guns • Wake Me Up When September Ends • When I Come Around • and more.
00103074 ....$12.99

Guitar Chord Songbook White Pages
400 songs in over 1,000 pages! Includes: California Girls • Footloose • Hey Jude • King of the Road • Man in the Mirror • and many more.
00702609................................$29.99

Irish Songs
45 Irish favorites: Danny Boy • Girl I Left Behind Me • Harrigan • I'll Tell Me Ma • The Irish Rover • My Wild Irish Rose • When Irish Eyes Are Smiling • and more!
00701044 ....$14.99

Billy Joel
60 Billy Joel favorites: • It's Still Rock and Roll to Me • The Longest Time • Piano Man • She's Always a Woman • Uptown Girl • We Didn't Start the Fire • You May Be Right • and more.
00699632 ....$15.99

Elton John
60 songs: Bennie and the Jets • Candle in the Wind • Crocodile Rock • Goodbye Yellow Brick Road • Pinball Wizard • Sad Songs (Say So Much) • Tiny Dancer • Your Song • and more.
00699732 ....$15.99

Ray LaMontagne
20 songs: Empty • Gossip in the Grain • Hold You in My Arms • I Still Care for You • Jolene • Trouble • You Are the Best Thing • and more.
00130337................................$12.99

Latin Songs
60 favorites: Bésame Mucho (Kiss Me Much) • The Girl from Ipanema (Garôta De Ipanema) • The Look of Love • So Nice (Summer Samba) • and more.
00700973 ....$14.99

Love Songs
65 romantic ditties: Baby, I'm-A Want You • Fields of Gold • Here, There and Everywhere • Let's Stay Together • Never My Love • The Way We Were • more!
00701043................................$14.99

Bob Marley
36 songs: Buffalo Soldier • Get up Stand Up • I Shot the Sheriff • Is This Love • No Woman No Cry • One Love • Redemption Song • and more.
00701704................................$12.99

Bruno Mars
15 hits: Count on Me • Grenade • If I Knew • Just the Way You Are • The Lazy Song • Locked Out of Heaven • Marry You • Treasure • When I Was Your Man • and more.
00125332 ....$12.99

Paul McCartney
60 from Sir Paul: Band on the Run • Jet • Let 'Em In • Maybe I'm Amazed • No More Lonely Nights • Say Say Say • Take It Away • With a Little Luck • more!
00385035 ....$16.95

Steve Miller
33 hits: Dance Dance Dance • Jet Airliner • The Joker • Jungle Love • Rock'n Me • Serenade from the Stars • Swingtown • Take the Money and Run • and more.
00701146................................$12.99

Modern Worship
80 modern worship favorites: All Because of Jesus • Amazed • Everlasting God • Happy Day • I Am Free • Jesus Messiah • and more.
00701801 ....$16.99

Motown
60 Motown masterpieces: ABC • Baby I Need Your Lovin' • I'll Be There • Stop! In the Name of Love • You Can't Hurry Love • more.
00699734 ....$16.95

The 1950s
80 early rock favorites: High Hopes • Mister Sandman • Only You (And You Alone) • Put Your Head on My Shoulder • Tammy • That's Amoré • and more.
00699922 ....$14.99

The 1980s
80 hits: Centerfold • Come on Eileen • Don't Worry, Be Happy • Got My Mind Set on You • Sailing • Should I Stay or Should I Go • Sweet Dreams (Are Made of This) • more.
00700551 ....$16.99

Nirvana
40 songs: About a Girl • Come as You Are • Heart Shaped Box • The Man Who Sold the World • Smells like Teen Spirit • You Know You're Right • and more.
00699762 ....$16.99

Roy Orbison
38 songs: Blue Bayou • Oh, Pretty Woman • Only the Lonely (Know the Way I Feel) • Working for the Man • You Got It • and more.
00699752 ....$12.95

For more information, see your local music dealer or visit www.halleonard.com

Peter, Paul & Mary
43 favorites: If I Had a Hammer (The Hammer Song) • Leaving on a Jet Plane • Puff the Magic Dragon • This Land Is Your Land • and more.
00103013 .... $12.99

Tom Petty
American Girl • Breakdown • Don't Do Me like That • Free Fallin' • Here Comes My Girl • Into the Great Wide Open • Mary Jane's Last Dance • Refugee • Runnin' Down a Dream • The Waiting • more.
00699883 .... $15.99

Pop/Rock
80 chart hits: Against All Odds • Come Sail Away • Every Breath You Take • Hurts So Good • Kokomo • More Than Words • Smooth • Summer of '69 • and more.
00699538 .... $14.95

Praise and Worship
80 favorites: Agnus Dei • He Is Exalted • I Could Sing of Your Love Forever • Lord, I Lift Your Name on High • More Precious Than Silver • Open the Eyes of My Heart • Shine, Jesus, Shine • and more.
00699634 .... $14.99

Elvis Presley
60 hits: All Shook Up • Blue Suede Shoes • Can't Help Falling in Love • Heartbreak Hotel • Hound Dog • Jailhouse Rock • Suspicious Minds • Viva Las Vegas • more.
00699633 .... $14.95

Queen
40 hits: Bohemian Rhapsody • Crazy Little Thing Called Love • Fat Bottomed Girls • Killer Queen • Tie Your Mother Down • Under Pressure • You're My Best Friend • and more!
00702395 .... $12.99

Rascal Flatts
23 Rascal Flatts hits: Bless the Broken Road • Easy • Here • Life Is a Highway • My Wish • Summer Nights • What Hurts the Most • Why Wait • and more.
00130951 .... $12.99

Red Hot Chili Peppers
50 hits: Californication • Give It Away • Higher Ground • Love Rollercoaster • Scar Tissue • Suck My Kiss • Under the Bridge • and more.
00699710 .... $16.95

Rock Ballads
54 songs: Amanda • Boston • Brick • Landslide • Love Hurts • Mama, I'm Coming Home • She Will Be Loved • Waiting for a Girl like You • and more.
00701034 .... $14.99

Rock 'n' Roll
80 rock 'n' roll classics: At the Hop • Great Balls of Fire • It's My Party • La Bamba • My Boyfriend's Back • Peggy Sue • Stand by Me • more.
00699535 .... $14.95

Bob Seger
41 favorites: Against the Wind • Hollywood Nights • Katmandu • Like a Rock • Night Moves • Old Time Rock & Roll • You'll Accomp'ny Me • and more!
00701147 .... $12.99

Carly Simon
Nearly 40 classic hits, including: Anticipation • Haven't Got Time for the Pain • Jesse • Let the River Run • Nobody Does It Better • You're So Vain • and more.
00121011 .... $14.99

Singer/Songwriter Songs
40 songs: Angel • Fields of Gold • Fifty Ways to Leave Your Lover • Hallelujah • Love Story • Maggie May • Rocky Mountain High • Strong Enough • Taxi • and more.
00126053 .... $14.99

Sting
50 favorites from Sting and the Police: Don't Stand So Close to Me • Every Breath You Take • Fields of Gold • King of Pain • Message in a Bottle • Roxanne • more.
00699921 .... $14.99

Taylor Swift
27 tunes: Fifteen • Hey Stephen • Love Story • Our Song • Picture to Burn • Tim McGraw • Today Was a Fairytale • White Horse • You Belong with Me • and more.
00701799 .... $15.99

Three Chord Acoustic Songs
30 acoustic songs: All Apologies • Blowin' in the Wind • Hold My Hand • Just the Way You Are • Ring of Fire • Shelter from the Storm • This Land Is Your Land • and more.
00123860 .... $14.99

Three Chord Songs
65 includes: All Right Now • La Bamba • Lay Down Sally • Mony, Mony • Rock Around the Clock • Rock This Town • Werewolves of London • You Are My Sunshine • and more.
00699720 .... $12.95

HAL•LEONARD®

Today's Hits
40 of today's top hits, including: Blurred Lines • Call Me Maybe • Cruise • Drive By • Ho Hey • Little Talks • Mirrors • Radioactive • Stay • We Are Young • When I Was Your Man • and more.
00120983 .... $14.99

Top 100 Hymns
100 songs: 'Tis So Sweet to Trust in Jesus • A Mighty Fortress Is Our God • Christ the Lord Is Risen Today • Higher Ground • In the Sweet by and By • Rock of Ages, Cleft for Me • and many more!
75718017 .... $14.99

Two-Chord Songs
Nearly 60 songs: ABC • Brick House • Eleanor Rigby • Fever • Paperback Writer • Ramblin' Man Tulsa Time • When Love Comes to Town • and more.
00119236 .... $14.99

Ultimate-Guitar
100 must-know songs: American Girl • Born This Way • Don't Look Back in Anger • Every Rose Has Its Thorn • Forget You • Hey Jude • Jackson • Rehab • Shout • Thriller • and more.
00702617 .... $24.99

U2
40 U2 songs: Beautiful Day • Mysterious Ways • New Year's Day • One • Sunday Bloody Sunday • Walk On • Where the Streets Have No Name • With or Without You • and more.
00137744 .... $14.99

Wedding Songs
50 songs that every gigging musician should know, including: Endless Love • Have I Told You Lately • Longer • Through the Years • and more.
00701005 .... $14.99

Hank Williams
68 classics: Cold, Cold Heart • Hey, Good Lookin' • Honky Tonk Blues • I'm a Long Gone Daddy • Jambalaya (On the Bayou) • Your Cheatin' Heart • and more.
00700607 .... $14.99

Stevie Wonder
40 of Stevie's best: For Once in My Life • Higher Ground • Isn't She Lovely • My Cherie Amour • Sir Duke • Superstition • Uptight (Everything's Alright) • Yester-Me, Yester-You, Yesterday • and more!
00120862 .... $14.99

Neil Young
35 songs: After the Gold Rush • Cinnamon Girl • Down by the River • Harvest • Heart of Gold • Like a Hurricane • Long May You Run • Ohio • Old Man • Southern Man • and more.
00700464 .... $14.99

Complete contents listings available online at www.halleonard.com

Prices, contents and availability subject to change without notice.